MW00781990

BONSAI WASN'T REALLY THAT BIG OF A HILL

One Man's Walk toward God

Pat McCool

ISBN 978-1-64258-541-4 (paperback)
ISBN 978-1-64258-543-8 (hardcover)
ISBN 978-1-64258-542-1 (digital)

Christian Faith Publishing, Inc.
832 Park Avenue
Meadville, PA 16335
www.christianfaithpublishing.com

Printed in the United States of America

Contents

CHAPTER 1

AND ... HERE WE GO

I didn't know at the time why I did it. I just remember looking at the sinks in the bathroom of my first grade class in Fort Lee, Virginia. I walked over to the first sink, put the stopper in the drain, and turned the water on. Then I did the same to the four remaining sinks. I strolled back into the classroom, sat down at my desk, and went back to coloring monkeys.

About ten minutes later, my teacher glanced toward the back of the room with a concerned look on her face. Water was seeping under the door into the classroom. She walked to the bathroom to find five overflowing sinks and the floor covered with water. It didn't take them long to clean it up, and for some reason there was no intensive manhunt to find the culprit. So I got away with it. This was not good.

A couple of months later, a letter arrived in the mail. It was a letter that would change my life. We all have moments that change our lives, and they usually don't happen at a preconceived time or highly anticipated event. They happen on a random Tuesday at four thirty in the afternoon when you're not expecting it. The letter was my father's new assignment. He was going to Vietnam. We were going to Mississippi.

Packing up and moving is a common occurrence for a military brat. It's just what you do. You live on one post for a year. You make friends, go to school, and get adjusted. Then *boom*, you pack up the station wagon, wave good-bye to your friends, and head across the country.

We would stop at a roadside park for a sandwich, pull over on the side of the highway a couple of times so my dad could beat the fire out of me and my brother, Mike, then roll into the next town.

By the time we left Virginia, I had lived in Fort Benning, Georgia; Hattiesburg, Mississippi; Fort Sill, Oklahoma; and Bad Kissingen, Germany. I had ridden the gondolas in Venice, climbed the Leaning Tower of Pisa, and posed for a picture wearing lederhosen and a sailor's hat in front of Michelangelo's statue. I wasn't nearly as amused by the things I had seen and their cultural significance as I was by my grandmother turning purple and throwing up in the gondola or my grandfather ordering food in an Italian restaurant. He glanced at the menu written in Italian, looked up at the waiter, and said "I'll have a bologna sandwich, and Sally here will have a Milk of Magnesia."

We moved to Moss Point, Mississippi where my dad grew up. My grandparents, aunts and uncles, and all of my cousins on my dad's side of the family lived there. It was a sad time because my dad was on the other side of the world, but living in Moss Point was a blast. My grandmother Sally McCool was the funniest woman I've ever known. She was a large woman with the vocal cords to match, and my cousins Ricky and JJ could make a funeral service burst into laughter. Spending a year and a half around these people removed any mystery of where my sense of humor came from.

We moved into a house my grandmother had picked out for us in downtown Moss Point. When I first laid eyes on this thing a shiver went down my spine. It looked like the house they used for the original set of *Bates Motel*. It was an old Civil War–era house with creaking wooden floors and hidden walls in the attic, a perfect place for the spooks I was sure were there, to hide while they waited for the sun to go down. If that wasn't enough to keep the covers over my head at night, the abandoned house across the street—formerly the home to Carl E. Lee, Robert E. Lee's brother—had broken windows and was covered with weeds. I was certain that Satan himself had spent time there. I would lay in bed all night with my eyes wide open, waiting for the creature from the black lagoon to crawl through my window.

Fortunately, I wasn't the only one who was freaked out by this place. My mother didn't put her foot down often, but when she did, things got handled. After two weeks in that horror house, she told my dad, "Max, this house is giving us the creeps and if you don't get us another place we're going to a hotel." Two weeks later we moved into a brand-new house in Riverwood subdivision.

Two weeks after that, Mom and Dad loaded me and my brother, Mike, into the station wagon and headed for the airport in Mobile, Alabama. Something was odd about this because Mom was driving. She rarely drove if my dad was with us. It wasn't until we got to the airport that we figured out why he was in the passenger seat. She stopped the car, and they both looked at each other with a look of seriousness that I hadn't seen before. They stared at each other for a moment until their eyes started welling up with tears.

He looked back at me, and my brother and said, "Now y'all behave yourselves and take care of your mother." He hugged and kissed her and said something under his breath we couldn't hear. He straightened himself up and said, "Okay, Polly," then got out of the car and walked through the fence leading to the plane that would take him away. That's when it dawned on us—we wouldn't see him again until this time the following year.

It didn't take long for us to adjust to him being gone, and life got good again. Most people in Moss Point knew my family, and my brother and I were fairly popular at Carl E. Lee elementary school. Within a few weeks of starting school, I had become the leader of my own schoolyard gang. We would form up at recess and slowly take our individual places behind trees on the playground. The other gang from the class next to ours would do the same. We would move stealthily from tree to tree until we were in the middle of the play-ground and have a "bro off" until the bell rang.

Once one of the other gang's scouts got a little too far behind enemy lines and we caught him. I had a small lock that I always kept in my pocket for moments such as this. We locked the kid by his belt loop to the fence at the back of the playground. The only way for him to get free was to tear his pants or take them off. He wasn't going anywhere. The bell rang, and we all ran back to class, leaving the poor kid locked to the fence. It didn't take long for a teacher to rescue him, and for some reason they weren't that concerned with finding the perps that locked him to the fence. There was a tap on the classroom door, and my teacher stepped out for a minute. She stepped back in and asked the class, "Does anybody know how Tommy Burns got locked to the fence?" My troops clammed up like hardened members of the mob. I realized at that moment I might have some leadership skills, but I was using them for no good.

My oldest brother, Jim, became a star on the Moss Point High School football team. He was one of their best players, and my grandmother was his biggest fan. She would sit in the middle of the bleachers and scream at the officials from the opening kickoff until the final whistle. She would use every curse word that a fine upstanding member of the First Baptist Church of Moss Point, Mississippi could get away with. The team was horrible, and I think they only won one game, but she was worth the price of admission.

While my grandmother's antics at football games were legendary, they were not her finest hour. That came when my other older brother, Mike, got sued by a neighbor for knocking his kid's teeth out with a Coke bottle. He had a bad habit of hurling solid objects at people, and I have the stitch scars on my forehead to prove it. I can only imagine what my dad was thinking when he got this news. Wait, what? I'm over here dodging bullets and I'm getting sued by some toothless kid?

Well court day arrived and Sally led our entourage into the courtroom ready for battle. The now toothless kid started the fight and my brother had just given him a little Jackson County justice. All that was left was to explain that to the judge, have him dismiss the case and taunt the kid's dad as we victoriously walked out of the courtroom. It was a great plan, but it didn't quite go that way. The tide started turning. The judge said one thing too many that my grandmother didn't like, and she sprang into action. She jumped to her feet and laid into him with the best Al Pacino impression I've ever seen. No, it didn't work. The judge slapped her with a contempt charge, threw her out of the courtroom, and we lost the case.

The day finally arrived. Dad was coming home. It was all my birthdays and Christmases rolled into one. My brother Mike and I were riding on the back of Steve Buyers' riding lawn mower when he rounded the corner in his yellow Corvair. We jumped off and sprinted to the house, and the party was on. He had brought a duffle bag full of goodies for both of us. The biggest prize was the jungle camouflage fatigues worn by the Green Berets and Australian Ranger hats. We put them on, hopped on our Western Auto Speed Racer bikes with wheelie bars on the back, and headed down the street to gloat. We road up and down the street, popping wheelies and firing our Mattel imitation M-16s at all our friends. We were the kings that day, and all the kids in the hood were our subjects.

Dad didn't spend any time in combat when he was in Vietnam, but he wasn't immune to dealing with its consequences. He was the liaison officer for the American and Australian troops, so he spent most of his time in Saigon at MACV headquarters. One day, a new arrival showed up in his office. He was an eighteen-year-old kid named Bobby Thornton, the son of one of my dad's good friends from Officers Candidate School. They talked for a while, and dad encouraged him and told him if he ever needed anything to let him know. About two weeks later, my dad was walking through the area where the body bags were laid to wait transfer back to Dover Air Force Base. As he passed the last bag, he glanced down at the toe tag. It read, "R. Thornton." It was his friend's son.

That story was the only time I heard him speak about the war, but there was another occasion when I saw the effect it had on him. He was sitting in the living room by himself one night watching *Platoon*. This was odd because he never watched movies about Vietnam, at least not when anyone was around. I had walked into the kitchen behind him, so he didn't know I was there. He was staring intently at the TV and seemed to be talking to himself. As I stepped into the room, I could see his face, and it became clear what he was saying. Tears were streaming down his face, and he kept repeating, "They did everything we asked them to do . . . they did everything we asked them to do." I quietly slipped out of the room and left him alone.

It wasn't long after Dad's return that the next letter came. He was being promoted to lieutenant colonel, and we were heading to Fort Leavenworth, Kansas so he could attend the United States Army Command and General Staff College. Becoming a lieutenant colonel in the United States Army was quite an accomplishment for somebody who enlisted as a buck private. In the 1950s, there were four ways to become an army officer. You either went to college, a military academy, got a battlefield commission, or busted your butt so you stood out enough to be invited to Officers Candidate School. My dad did the latter.

My father's family wasn't exactly poor, but my grandfather had to raise five kids on a fireman's salary, so there wasn't some pile of cash sitting around to pay for college. Times were different then. You didn't take out $200,000 in student loans and get a liberal arts degree while you figured out what your life's passion was. You either had the money to go or you didn't. Dad did get two years paid for on a football scholarship at Mississippi Gulf Coast Junior College where his team won a national championship. After that, the choices weren't that great in Jackson County. His best options were going to work at the paper mill for International Paper or the shipyard for Ingall's Ship Building. He enlisted in the army, worked hard, and took classes in his spare time. He got the education he needed to advance and was now two promotions away from general.

CHAPTER 2

BONSAI!

We pulled into the officer's quarters at Fort Leavenworth in the summer of 1969. There was a group of kids playing on the block, so we unloaded the station wagon and headed out to meet them. We immediately made friends and started up a game of baseball in the field next to where we lived. The field was perfect for baseball because it had a creek that served as the outfield fence. If you hit it in the creek it was a home run or what we called a "creeker." I never got one in there, but my brother, Mike, would fill it up. Home plate was a tall pole with a massive speaker/horn on top that would deafen you if a tornado or nuclear missile was heading our way. Kansas was in tornado alley, and there were silos on the base that previously had live missiles in them.

This was the middle of the Cold War, so there was always the chance the Soviets would target the base if war broke out. We didn't walk around in fear of a missile attack, but if you lived on an army base at the time, you definitely thought about it. I only heard the horn go off once, and that was enough for me. I was walking across the field by myself when a major storm blew in. I started getting pelted by golf-ball-sized hail, so I began sprinting toward my house at full throttle. That's when the horn went off and knocked me to the ground. I don't know what hurt worse—the large chunks of ice putting lumps on my noggin or that horn bursting my eardrums.

A few days later, we organized a tent sleepover in our backyard. All our new friends from the block came over, including the cute thirteen-year-old girl from across the street. We were playing cards and eating hot dogs when out of the blue she suggested we play strip poker. Whoa, wait a minute. Did she mean the kind of strip poker that might lead to me seeing something that the closest I had gotten to was reading the Sears catalog? Yes, she did, so every boy in that tent sat up straight and got their game face on. She started dealing, and we started losing. This wasn't going the way we had hoped, but eventually the moment came. She lost a hand.

Our eyes lit up like Christmas morning as we stared with great anticipation to see what was coming off first. Words can't describe the dejection we all felt as she casually reached up and pulled a hair pin out of her hair and tossed it on the blanket. We had been had. She had about twenty of those things in her hair and that was all that was coming off. Worse yet, some of us were getting perilously close to a personal moment of truth ourselves and we didn't have hair pins to rely on. I was one bad hand away from everybody knowing that my tighty-whities were one size too big and had a large mustard stain on them. Then, in what could only have been an act of God, it started pouring rain. The tent started drooping and was about to collapse, so we all bolted toward our houses.

Things were looking up. We already had a group of friends and received a great lesson on the deviousness of the female mind. Then the moving vans started showing up. One by one our new friends piled into their station wagons and headed out of town. Turns out we had gotten to our new assignment a little early and they hadn't left for theirs. They weren't our new friends. We were their replacements.

It wasn't long after the last van rolled out that the new ones started showing up. The first to arrive was my next-door neighbor, an eight-year-old kid who was the same age as me, John Alley. His father would eventually become one of the highest-ranking admirals in the United States Navy. Fort Leavenworth was an army base, but members of all branches would come there to attend the Command and General Staff College, which Dad was attending. The next kid was ten years old, the same age as my brother. I don't remember his last name, but I'll never forget his first. His name was Steve. The union between Steve and my brother Mike would bring me one excruciatingly painful moment after another.

The two of them were constantly devising new inventions and trying experiments. I was their crash test dummy. The first experiment taught me that Mary Poppins was a fraud. You cannot float to the ground with an umbrella. "Come on, man, jump!" Mike said. The words "come on, man" were usually the last words I heard before I ended up bursting into tears.

Steve chimed in, "Make sure you clear the awning."

"You sure this is gonna work?" I yelled down from the roof.

"Of course it's gonna work!" Mike yelled. "You saw the movie."

It didn't. The umbrella collapsed, and I plummeted to the earth faster than the apple that hit Isaac Newton's head. I sprained an ankle and almost bit my tongue in half.

One of their more sophisticated inventions was the parachute they made out of a bed sheet with kite strings they attached to the back of Mike's bike. Yep, they were going to let me try it first. This looked good on paper, and I was actually happy to be the first to try it. I mean, it's a parachute, what could possibly go wrong? I hopped on Mike's bike and pulled out on Kearney Boulevard and up to the top of what we called Kearney Hill that ran down beside our quarters.

"No, not Kearney," they shouted. "Kearney's not steep enough for the chute to open."

"Well, where am I gonna do it?" I asked.

They both slowly turned toward the hill that rose up from the bottom of Kearney and climbed all the way to the noncommissioned officers quarters at the top.

It was a massive hill with a steep incline, so tall that people at the top looked like ants. It had a reputation and a name that evoked terror in the neighborhood. It was called Bonsai! Now I was about to go down it. I peddled up as far as I could, stopping about halfway to walk the bike to the top. I pointed the bike to the bottom of the hill, climbed on, and waited for instructions.

Mike yelled from the bottom of the hill, "Start when I say go and peddle as fast as you can."

So, when the time was right, he would scream pull and I was then supposed to yank the string attached to the parachute. "Go!" he shouted, and I took off.

I peddled as fast as I could, and by the time I was half way down the hill I'm flying. Then they shouted in harmony, "Pull, pull, pull!" So I did.

It worked masterfully. The sheet filled with air and stopped that bike cold. There was only one plot hole in this horror film I was starring in. It stopped the bike, but it didn't stop me. I went hurtling down that hill in a heap of torn flesh and bruised bones until I rolled to a merciful stop at the bottom. I laid there in agony as they jumped up and down celebrating their victory.

"It worked, it worked!" they shouted, but for some reason they decided not to try it themselves. That wasn't the last time I got suckered into one of their schemes, but it was the last time I went down Bonsai. The other kids had a lot of fun riding up and down it without getting hurt. Of course they didn't have a sadistic brother attach a bed sheet to their bike, but that didn't matter. That hill had hurt me, and I learned the best way to make sure it didn't hurt me again was to stop going down it. This was a lesson I didn't need to learn.

CHAPTER 3

REALLY, DAD, JUST TO SAVE FIFTY CENTS?

The school year was about to start, and it was time for our first haircuts on our new base. Now if you were an army brat in 1969, there wasn't a lot of mystery as to what this haircut was going to look like. You would have just enough hair on the sides of your head to feel it and just enough on top to make it flat. It would be so flat and firm you could carry your books on it. The mystery was where he was going to take us to get it cut. We didn't see this coming. There are two prisons at Leavenworth. One is the federal prison that everyone has heard about, which has housed some of the most notorious prisoners in the country. The other one is a military prison for housing people who commit crimes while on active duty. While it is not as foreboding as the famous one, there are still some scary characters there. They had an annex with shops at the prison where inmates could work and learn a trade while they did their time.

One of the shops at the military prison was a barbershop. You could save fifty cents off the regular price of a haircut on the post if you went to the prison. Of course you had to not be bothered by having a guy that was shackled to the floor and serving fifteen to life whack away on you with a pair of scissors. The guy standing in the corner with the loaded M-16 made it only slightly more comforting. To me, this was taking being a cheapskate to an unnecessary level. I didn't find out until later on that Dad did it to support the prisoners. Once a week while we were stationed there, he would go to the prison to counsel the inmates. I always thought it was part of his duty. It wasn't. He did it on his own because he wanted to encourage the guys and help them get their lives on track. That's just who he was. To him they were soldiers and he loved every one of them.

School finally started, and I was in third grade. The school was only two blocks away, so I could walk. At lunch time, I would walk home and eat a sandwich, watch *Let's Make a Deal* and the first half of *Dark Shadows*, then head back to school. When it snowed, I would drag my sled to school and sled home on the way back. My teacher was Mrs. McClanahan, and she had a flair for teaching history. She read us the story of Lewis and Clark in a way that made you feel like you were with them on the journey. When she finished the book, she challenged all the students in the class to a contest. We would read a book and do a book report on it. Whomever read the most books and did the most reports by Christmas break would win a prize. I was first out of the gate. I was only in the third grade, so I didn't plow into anything by Hemingway or Faulkner. I opted for Henry Huggins, big letters and double spacing with drawings of the characters on every other page. It didn't matter though. It was a book.

I read the book and wrote a report on it. I brought it in the following Monday, and the teacher lit up. She was happy that someone had taken her up on the contest. She pulled out a certificate with printed circles on it and stuck a shiny gold sticker on the first circle. She then printed my name on it in bold letters and hung it on the wall for everybody to see. I was all teeth as I sat at my desk and beamed. While these other losers had spent their weekend chasing grasshoppers, I had applied myself and I was getting my just reward. The week passed and instead of reading another book, I decided I would just soak in the adulation a while longer and read another book when I felt like it.

Then the following Monday came. She calls the roll, and Betsy Johnson sitting two seats in front of me raises her hand. Mrs. McClanahan called on her, and the words thundered out of her mouth.

"I have a book report," Betsy said.

"You do?" Mrs. McClanahan replied.

"Yes, ma'am, I have three of them," Betsy replied.

I thought to myself, hang on a minute, I ain't buying this. No way this bifocaled kid has read three books and done a report on them in one weekend. Well, she did and she had a certificate with three gold stickers on the wall to prove it. I was crushed! My glory was stolen. She had three stickers, and I only had one. It was decision time. How was I going to handle this? My first option was to go home, get busy, and teach this kid who ruled that classroom. My second was to act like I didn't care, book reports were for sissies anyway, and never do another one. I chose option two. A trend was starting to form.

A few weeks into the school year football season started, and if you were a McCool, you played. As a matter of fact, we played every sport that was available—football, baseball, basketball, and track. If there had been a badminton team, we would have been on that too. My oldest brother, Jim, actually played a sport in Germany called push ball. It was this huge ball about five feet tall, and each team would get on either side of it and push until one team got it across the goal line. Not a whole lot of strategy involved but it looked like a lot of fun.

Mike had reached the age where he could play football, but I wasn't old enough yet, so I joined the local boxing club. We practiced on Saturday morning and had a match at the end of each month. I wasn't that happy about missing my favorite cartoons, *Dastardly and Muttley in their Flying Machines* and *Cool McCool*, but I turned out to be a pretty good boxer. I won my first bout fairly easily, but a problem was developing at practice. The coach kept making me fight this kid who was a year older and a lot bigger. This wasn't going well for me at all. The bell would ring, and then he would pummel me until it rang again.

One day I asked the coach why he kept picking me to fight Sasquatch. He said I was the only one that would give him a fight. I assume his idea of "giving him a fight" was me repeatedly striking his boxing glove with my face. One day, he hit me so hard I got that blast of ammonia smell that football players have when they get their bell rung. I hadn't had that smell since I tried to chug a bottle of

Mr. Clean at the grocery store and had to be rushed to the hospital to have my stomach pumped. This was it for me. I was done. Dad wouldn't let me quit, so I feigned some kind of minor illness every Saturday morning until the season ended. Once again, when things got a little rough, I quit. This was becoming a habit.

As football season was coming to an end, the annual Punt, Pass, and Kick competition was held. Kids in each age group from seven to fourteen would punt, pass, and place-kick a football. The distance of each one would be measured then the yardage would be added. The top three participants would win the gold, silver, and bronze trophies. The winner of the gold trophy would go on to the state competition at a Kansas City Chief's game. I was jacked. I spent half of my free time passing, punting, and kicking a football. I knew I was coming home with some hardware.

The first event was the Pass. I sailed a perfect spiral right down the middle of the field. The next event was Punt. Once again, I launched a perfect spiral with just the right amount of hang time to get it down the field. I was watching my competition, and nobody had matched me in the first two events. There was one kid who was about a foot taller than everybody else who was hanging with me, but I was still ahead of him. The gold trophy and a trip to Kansas City was mine for the taking. All I had to do was nail a respectable place-kick and I was on my way. I placed the ball on the tee and walked back five steps. I started toward the ball with the intention of just getting off a good solid kick. Just as I was about to put my foot in it, I decided to crush it. Bad move! I hit the side of the ball, and it rolled about ten yards and spun to a halt.

I was in shock. My first chance at glory, and I had pulled a massive choke job. I slinked off the field and headed to the bleachers where Mike and Dad were waiting. My dad cheered me up by pointing out that my distance in the pass and punt might be enough for the bronze or silver trophy. I would still get to stand on the podium, get my name called over the loud speaker, and receive the adulation I so desperately craved. They totaled up the scores and announced the winners. I was not one of them. My dad called my mom to come pick me up as he and Mike had to stay for Mike's events, which were about to start. He knew I was beaten, and I needed to leave. A few minutes later, my mom pulled up and took me home to sulk in silence.

A couple of hours later, Mike and Dad came in the door screaming my name, "Pat, Pat, Pat!" I came down stairs to see what the commotion was about. "You won the bronze, you won the bronze!" they exclaimed.

"Wait, what are you talking about?" I asked. "What do you mean I won the bronze?"

They said there was a kid in my event who had participated in the wrong age group so he wasn't eligible to win, so I had won third place. Now I had several emotions going on inside of me. I was happy because I actually won a trophy. I was also steamed because I didn't get my recognition, and confused, because if I had won, I wondered where the heck was my trophy? It turns out the officials at the event didn't want to hurt the other kid's feelings, so they didn't tell him he was disqualified and let him keep the trophy. I was mad then. I lost my moment in the sun, and this kid got to keep his because he either blatantly cheated or had the most ignorant parents in the whole town of Leavenworth, Kansas.

A few weeks later, the day came to go down to the Ford dealership where all the winners would get their picture taken with their trophies. This was a big deal because that picture was going on the front page of the local newspaper. There was only one problem. I didn't have a trophy. They let the cheater keep mine so they had to order a new one for me, but it hadn't arrived in time for the picture. Once again, my moment of glory had turned to humiliation because I was the only one there without a trophy. Nobody even knew why I was there. I was hoping they would make an announcement so everybody would know why I was there. "By the way, the kid with the cowlicks and the flattop on the back row actually won the bronze trophy." They didn't, because they obviously didn't want to hurt the kid's feelings who had no business being there. My anger only increased when I got a good look at him. I'm thinking, who in their right mind wouldn't know this punk wasn't eight years old? He was a foot taller than everybody else, had a mustache, and looked old enough to be test driving cars at the dealership before the rest of us got there.

The rest of the year flew by, and it turned out to be one of the best of my life. We were only a thirty-minute ride from Kansas City, and Dad took us to several Kansas City Royals baseball games. I also became a huge fan of the Kansas City Chiefs football team and got to meet some of the players at a charity basketball game. They would go on to win the Super Bowl the following year. I survived all of Mike and his friend Steve's attempts to kill me. The massive outbreak of poison ivy I had on my butt cheeks had finally cleared up too. Mike and Steve convinced me that a poison ivy plant was actually aloe vera and it would sooth the rash I had gotten from hiking through the woods on a hot day. It wasn't and it didn't. I did learn a valuable lesson on how to scratch your rear end in public. It involved leaning against the corner of a building while acting like you're tying your shoe. It's a lesson that has served me well to this day.

Dad's new assignment had come. He was being stationed at the Pentagon, so we were to move to Washington, D.C. This time, though, there was a twist. It was a twist that would change everything in my life from that point forward. Most of us have moments like this in our lives, but we don't realize it at the time. We weren't going to Washington, D.C. after all, and I am so fortunate we didn't. Had we gone, I wouldn't know all the people I love so dearly and thank God for every day.

My oldest brother, Jim, had stayed in Moss Point when we moved to Kansas. He lived with my grandparents while he finished his senior year of high school. He was now heading ninety miles up the road to Hattiesburg, Mississippi to play football at the University of Southern Mississippi. My dad wanted to be there to watch him play, so he got his orders changed. He was now going to teach in the ROTC department at USM where Jim was about to enroll. I don't know how he pulled this off, but I do know he had friends in high places. It wasn't uncommon to watch TV and see one of his friends. One of his good friends who was our neighbor in Germany ended up being the Chairman of the Joint Chiefs of Staff under Ronald

Reagan. However he did it, we were going back to Mississippi. It would be a long time before I moved again.

The week before we left, Jim flew up to join us. He was going to drive back with us because we were going through Beaumont, Texas to visit my mom's family. I was thrilled that Jim was coming. He was like a God to me. He was a football star and everything I wanted to be. On the second day he was there, he took me and Mike to a movie. This wasn't just any movie. This was *Easy Rider*, at the drive-in, which means I was going to see a movie that eight-year-old kids were not old enough to see. I had no idea what I was in for, but halfway through the movie, the moment came. Jim turned to me and Mike and said, "Close your eyes until I tell you to open them." No, that wasn't going to happen. We both sat straight up in our seats and stared intently to see what we weren't supposed to see. A moment later, there it was. A naked woman! Not some underwear model in the Sears Catalog or somebody in the *National Geographic* breastfeeding in the Congo. This was a bona fide bare naked girl. I now had a new interest, and it would be a motivating force over the next twenty years.

CHAPTER 4

YOU THOUGHT I SAID WHAT?

Two days later, moving day came and we headed towards Fort Sill, Oklahoma. Fort Sill was the home of the artillery, and Dad was an artilleryman, so he had to stop by to take care of some business. Mike had also been born there, so we passed by the hospital on our way out of town so he could see it. Just as we were driving off the post, I decided to try to be funny.

"There's a horror house at Fort Sill," I said.

"Oh, where?" my mother asked.

"Where Mike was born," I replied. Well, I had said "horror," but my dad had heard "whore." He slammed on the brakes and reached back and hit me in the face with his open hand. I was dazed and confused. I was dazed because this was the hardest I had been hit in my life. I was confused because I didn't know why I had been hit.

I started crying and asked, "Why did you do that?"

"You know why I did it," he replied. "Now shut up, I don't want to hear another word out of you." I didn't know why he had done it. I was eight years old and had never heard of a whore house. I also didn't know that our relationship was starting to change, but it was.

After a brief stop in Texas to visit with my mom's family, we rolled into Hattiesburg, Mississippi, the place where I would live for the next forty years. We bought a house on Brookwood Drive and moved in right before school started.

The first day of school came, and I put on my favorite Mickey Mouse T-shirt and hopped into the station wagon. I walked into my fourth grade class for the first time and immediately realized that this was going to be different. All the boys in the classroom looked like the Beatles, and I looked like a drill sergeant. This was 1970 and this was how kids who didn't live on army posts looked. I was embarrassed but figured it wouldn't take long for my hair to grow out and I would no longer look like Uncle Fester. I was wrong. Just as my hair started to grow out, Dad took us to Cook's Barber Shop. Mike and I begged for mercy, but it was to no avail. He plopped me into the chair and said, "Flat top, military style." Mr. Cook made one pass with the trimmer, and my eyes welled up. Dad didn't like that, so he had him make another pass. I'm now visibly crying, so he started laughing and had him keep cutting until I looked like a cue ball. Our relationship was changing indeed.

Hairstyles weren't the only thing that was different in Hattiesburg. This wasn't an army post and all these kids hadn't just met. They had grown up in the same neighborhood and knew each other since birth. They had already established their circle of friends, and I was just a new kid with a weird haircut. I was no longer one of the cool kids, but I did become friends with the kid sitting beside me. It turns out we had similar backgrounds, but it would be a while before I found that out. His name was Van Overstreet. He lived within walking distance of my house with his mother and four brothers.

I didn't know where Van's father was, and as it turned out, he didn't either. One day, Dad was driving us to the country club to go swimming. He asked Van what his father did, and Van said he was in the air force. My dad then asked him where he was. Van said, "I don't know," with a somber look on his face. Dad didn't say anything else, and I never brought it up again. Several months later, we were playing at his house and he pulled out an old copy of the *Washington Post*. On the front page in large bold letters, it read, "JETS MISSING OVER KOREA." The article said that US planes were flying near the North Korean border and had disappeared. No one knew for sure what had happened, but the North Koreans were suspected of shooting them down. It almost restarted the Korean War. Van's dad was flying one of those planes.

The union between Van and me would be the start of my path to juvenile delinquency. It began innocently enough. Van knew that they left the back door to the Saenger Theater open while the movies were playing. He devised a brilliant plan. We would sneak through the door and slip behind the curtains on the side of the theater. Then we would stealthily work our way to the back of the theater and take our seats. We could then use the money our parents gave us for tickets on Junior Mints and extra popcorn. We pulled this off several times before we were discovered by the assistant manager. We didn't get in trouble for it because the guy didn't actually catch us. He saw us as we were slipping behind the curtain and yelled for us to stand still. We quickly realized that he was about fifteen cheeseburgers away from being fast enough to catch us, so we took off running. We wouldn't be so lucky in the future.

Feeling emboldened by our escape at the movie theater, we decided to try shoplifting. As it turned out, we were pretty good at it. We started with stainless steel lighters, tobacco pipes, and playing cards. We soon got bored with that and graduated to record albums. The first album I made it out of the store with was Black Sabbath's *Paranoid*. Ironic because I would eventually play the guy, Ozzy Osbourne (whose picture was on the album cover), on the Biography Channel.

We were actually about to end our careers as master thieves because we had stolen about everything Eckerd's Drugstore had worth stealing. It was too late, though; they had caught on to us. When we went down for our last hoorah, they had a sting set up. A plain-clothed off-duty police officer was waiting to collar us. We perused the aisles, made our selection, and slipped out the door. We hid our "take" behind the store while we went to Baskin Robbins for some ice cream. When we returned to pick up our contraband, the off-duty cop jumped out from behind the dumpster. We were busted. I never thought I would throw away a chocolate mint ice cream cone from Baskin Robbins, but I suddenly lost my appetite. I remember it melting in the shopping cart I had smashed it into as they perp walked us to the squad car. We were nine years old, so they called our parents down to the police station to pick us up. My dad took me home and gave me an epic butt whipping. That was the end of my shoplifting career, but not the end of me getting into trouble.

For our next project we decided to try our hand at vandalism. Van lived two blocks south of the school we attended, and I lived four blocks to the north. We would meet at the school to start our day's adventures. About two weeks before the fifth grade started, we met at the school and Van had an idea. We were both dreading the start of the school year, and Van had figured out a way to delay it. He surmised that if we broke some of the windows out of what would be our fifth grade classroom, the start of the school year would be delayed while they replaced them. Sounded legit to me, so we picked up some rocks and started hurling. We would meet there every day and break a few windows before getting on with our day's business. This soon caught on in the neighborhood, and our other friends started doing it to their classrooms too.

It took about a week before our handiwork was noticed. By then, that side of the school looked like a burned out warehouse in the ghetto. Someone waited at the school until the next perpetrator showed up and nailed him as he launched his rock. He sang like a canary, and the roundup began. Van and I were the first to be hauled in. We sang too. The school's principal asked us each how many windows we had broken. Van answered first. He looked the principal right in the eye and calmly said, "One." The principal looked at me and asked me the same question. Without missing a beat, I confessed that I had also broken one. If he was going to let us off by copping to one instead of admitting we were the ring leaders, then that was the path I was taking. I got my obligatory butt whipping and had to do some community service at the school. The school year started as planned.

Even though Van instigated most of our troubles, his mother blamed me. She decided we could no longer be friends. I guess it was just as well because Van had a sadistic streak. He seemed to derive great pleasure from causing me pain. Once while spending the night with him, I awoke to a burning sensation on my legs and stomach. It seems Van had covered me with wooden matches and was methodically lighting them while I slept. That wasn't as bad as the time I awoke to painful stings on my back. I looked over to see a gun barrel sticking out between Van's mattress and pillows. He was shooting me with his BB gun. While those were painful, at least they weren't as lethal as the time he threw a live copperhead snake at me as I stepped into his backyard. We would get together from time to time throughout our lives. Our paths may have gone in different directions, but we always considered ourselves best friends.

Van died of cancer seven years ago. RIP Howard Claven Overstreet. I hope you finally found out what happened to your dad.

CHAPTER 5

HAVE YOU HEARD ABOUT YOUR BROTHER, JIM?

One by-product of my time as a petty thief was that I had amassed a nice album collection and a new passion. I decided I wanted to be a musician. The biggest obstacle I had to overcome was I had absolutely no musical talent. I wasn't going to let this stand in my way because I really had no interest in music. I had interest in getting girls, and being a rock star seemed to be the best way to accomplish that. So I formed a band. You didn't need to be able to play an instrument to join. We were an air band, so you just needed to be able to act like you could. I recruited four of the coolest kids in the neighborhood, and Pat McCool and the Harleys was born.

We would be a five piece, drums, keyboard, rhythm guitar, and tambourine. I, of course, was the singer and lead guitar player. My brother, Jim, had a set of drums and an electric guitar and amplifier. We used the drums and guitar, but had no use for the amplifier. I didn't need anybody hearing the awful sounds that were emanating from that guitar. We had a spare room in our house with a loud stereo set up as our studio. We would crank that stereo up as loud as it would go so you couldn't hear the horrible noise we were actually making. This would go on for hours until the woman next door beat on the front door of my house and shut us down.

After a few weeks of practicing our act, we were ready for our debut. We just needed a venue. I figured our school would be the best place. That's where the girls we wanted to impress were and that's what this was all about. I decided to hit up all the teachers in fourth grade until I found one willing to give us our big break. I skipped my homeroom teacher because she was a mean old woman with the disposition of Attila the Hun. The math teacher said no, and the history teacher just smiled and shook her head. My last hope was the English teacher, Mrs. Smith. She said yes, and it was on. Our concert would be at the end of English class on the Friday before the last week of school.

The day came, and I bounced out of bed. This was the day that all the kids in the fourth grade at W.I. Thames elementary would find out how cool I was. I gathered my troops up at the beginning of class and was hit with my first sign of trouble. My keyboard player was bailing on me. I didn't know if he had chickened out or wised up, but I decided to move on without him. If he didn't want to be on the cover of *Tiger Beat*, that was his problem. Then the second leak in the boat sprang. The tambourine player decided to follow the lead of the cowardly keyboard player and he bailed too. I'm starting to panic now, because if we lose one more guy, we become a duo. I had no intention of becoming Simon and Garfunkel when I had spent a month preparing to be Robert Plant. Fortunately, my drummer and guitar player stuck with me, so all I needed was to enlist a tambourine player. This shouldn't be hard because it doesn't take any practice to stand there and shake a tambourine.

The first kid I asked jumped all over it. I wasn't surprised. Who wouldn't want a last-minute shot at glory and to have all the girls in the fourth grade fawning over you? The crisis was averted. I had adapted, modified, and overcome. It was just a matter of letting the minutes on the clock tick away until show time.

Finally, the clock hit 1:50 and it was time to roll. Mrs. Smith wanted to see what I was going to play, so I showed her the three records I had to choose from: Iron Butterfly, Led Zeppelin, and the Partridge Family. She picked the Partridge Family. That was cool with me. I saw myself as more Robert Plant than David Cassidy, but David Cassidy was rolling in the women and that was all that mattered.

We put the record on the record player and took our positions. I did a three count and the drummer started the record. Three, two, one . . . oh my god! The third and fatal leak had sprung in the boat, and it was about to sink. I was in such a hurry to shoot to stardom before the end of the school year, I had forgotten the most important piece of equipment for an air band. A stereo loud enough to disguise our lack of talent. You could barely hear David Cassidy singing from the tiny speaker on the side of that record player. I turned as red as a Stop sign, and fluid started pouring from every gland in my body. We had two choices. We could start singing and playing and make total fools of ourselves, or we could stand there motionless and make total fools of ourselves. We took the second choice and just stood there frozen while everybody stared at us like we were some exhibit at the zoo. Finally, Mrs. Smith put us out of our misery.

"Maybe just a little more practice," she said.

"Um yeah, we'll work the kinks out and come back next year," I mumbled. That was the end of Pat McCool and the Harleys.

A week later, the school year came to a merciful end. It would be three months before I saw most of the kids who had witnessed my humiliation. Surely, they would have forgotten about it by then. My dream of becoming a heartthrob through music was crushed, so it was time to move to the next option, star athlete. A few weeks into the summer I competed in the Junior Olympics. I won the high jump and long jump and finished second in the 220-yard dash. It was now on to the state finals in Meridian, Mississippi.

My dad drove me to the meet, and we got to the stadium an hour before my first event. My mother had packed us lunch, and we were going to eat before the meet started. We sat in the back of the station wagon and started eating. About that time, I noticed a cute girl with whom I went to school sitting with her family across the parking lot. She seemed to be staring at me. For some reason, I felt embarrassed to be sitting in the back of a Ford Country Squire eating a potted meat sandwich. I asked Dad if I could go finish eating with my buddy Brent Swindall. Brent was the kid who won the 220-yard dash in which I finished second. The top two finishers in each event advanced to state, so we would be competing against each other later that day. Dad said no. I asked again. He said no again. I asked a third time. He said no again, but this time his no was accompanied by a loud voice and a smack to the head. I immediately looked to see if the cute girl had seen me get walloped. She had. Getting smacked in the head with mayonnaise on your face is far more embarrassing than being seen eating in the back of a Ford Country Squire. These unnecessary smackings were starting to take their toll, but I didn't have time to dwell on it. It was time for the high jump.

As the event started, the official asked us where we wanted to place the bar to start. Several kids suggested various heights. The height they settled on was one inch higher than anything I had previously cleared. I was doomed. I knew I was going to lose, but I wasn't surprised because I had actually cheated to win in Hattiesburg. The rules for the high jump require you to leave the ground on one foot, which means you can't dive over the bar. I did. They didn't say anything. I won and proudly accepted my first place ribbon on the podium.

Now I'm in Meridian and they are saying something. The last thing the official said was, "Remember, you have to leave the ground on one foot so, no diving." Beautiful, not only am I going to lose badly, but I'm not even going to be able to reach my best height because I can't cheat. I had to quickly try to remember how to Fosbury Flop. This was the proper technique for high jumping named after Dick Fosbury who invented it. My brother Jim had tried to teach me this while helping me train for the meet. He warned me that diving was illegal, but I didn't listen to him. It didn't matter anyway. These kids were better than me, and I couldn't have won if I'd had a pogo stick. My first jump was worse than expected. I landed right on the bar and bent it in half. The event had to be delayed for ten minutes while they found another bar. I didn't stick around for my second attempt.

I now head to the long jump; this is my event. I schooled the kids back in Hattiesburg, and Jim had worked with me for the last two weeks to perfect my technique. It was just a matter of nailing my three jumps and collecting my ribbon. I got to the long jump pit and noticed all of the kids there looked older than me. I told the official my name and asked where the line started. He looked up my name and said my event ended an hour ago. I asked him what he was talking about, and he said the nine-year-olds jumped an hour ago. This was the eleven-year-olds. My coach had given me the wrong start time. I thought, no problem, just let me knock out my three jumps and they could go inform the kid who thought he won that he hadn't. No dice, my event was finished and so were my hopes for gold in the long jump.

I had one last chance to avoid going home empty-handed, and it wasn't that promising. I had lost the 220-yard dash in Hattiesburg to my buddy Brent Swindall by a sizable margin. To make matters worse, we were competing against a kid we had been hearing about for weeks. He was supposed to be the fastest nine-year-old on the planet and the rest of us were just there to give him somebody to beat. He would eventually become a football star for Alabama and the Green Bay Packers. I lined up in the block next to Brent. "Flash Gordon" is in the block next to him. The starter fires the gun and we're off. The two of them immediately start pulling away from the pack. I know I'm not winning this thing but I didn't let up. It's my last event, and I'm going down swinging. When I got to the finish line, I saw Brent celebrating. He had smoked that kid whom everyone had come to see. When I crossed the finish line, Brent yelled, "Way to go, McCool." I thought he was just congratulating me on a good effort. What I didn't realize was that even though I had finished with the pack, I had been in the lead when I finished. That meant I finished in third place and won the blue ribbon. The fact that I didn't give up and quit had paid off. It was a lesson I should have remembered.

The summer passed, and it was time for the fifth grade. I was finally going to be able to play tackle football. After the first week of practice, I had earned a starting position. When the season began, I was the starting middle linebacker and defensive captain. We only won a couple of games, but I had a blast. I also got to see my brother play for the first time since we left Moss Point. Jim was playing for the Southern Miss junior varsity team, and they were playing Nicholls State in Thibodaux, Louisiana. We packed an ice chest and headed down for the game.

We pulled up to the stadium, and Dad asked a security guard how much the tickets were. He said, "I think five bucks." Dad being the cheapskate that he was thought that was a bit steep for a junior varsity (JV) game, so he asked the guy where the team entrance was.

He pointed to the gate, and we pulled up. He told the guy at the gate that he was the team doctor and needed to know how to get to their locker room. The guy not only let us in for free but let us drive into the stadium and park with the Southern Miss team buses.

As we got out of the car, one of the coaches noticed us and shouted, "Hey, Colonel." Everybody in Hattiesburg called Dad "The Colonel" and he was good friends with all the coaches at Southern Miss. We walked over to him, and Dad explained that he was the team doctor for this game. The coach started laughing and said, "Follow me." He took us over and introduced us to the athletic director of Nicholls State. The next thing I know, we are on our way up the elevator to the press box. The Nicholls State Athletic Director sat us in the coaches' box and asked us to let him know if we needed anything. Every few minutes, some kid would walk in bringing us free hot dogs, cokes, and popcorn.

Jim didn't play in the first quarter, but I was digging the red carpet treatment. Halfway through the second quarter, Dad noticed a phone sitting in front of me. He picked it up and said, "Let's see what this is connected to." A few moments later, one of the Southern Miss coaches picked up the other end. Dad cracked a joke about the preferential treatment we were getting and then said, "Hey, tell Henry to put McCool in." Henry was the name of the JV head coach. A few minutes later, Jim jogged onto the field. Jim played fullback in high school but was moved to tight end at Southern Miss. If he was going to get in on the action, they were going to have to throw it to him. By the start of the second half, Jim had played a lot but hadn't had a pass thrown to him. Dad picked up the phone again, and the same coach answered. Dad said, "Tell Henry to throw it to him." A couple of plays later, the phone in the press box rang. The coach on the other end said, "Watch this." On the next play, Jim ran a ten-yard curl across the middle. The QB threw a perfect strike, and he caught it and ran for another ten yards. We were ecstatic. He would catch four more passes and a touchdown before the game was over. It was the last time I would see him play.

Several months later, I was at a friend's house helping him with his paper route. We were folding the papers and putting the rubber bands on them. The door burst open, and it was Robby Brent. He was a friend of the kid's brother whom I was helping. He was also a friend of my brother Mike and knew our family well.

He said, "Your mother's looking for you. Have you heard about your brother, Jim?"

I said, "No, what are you talking about?" He took the paper I was folding out of my hands and opened it up. The headlines read, "TWO USM STUDENTS KILLED IN CAR CRASH." I was numb. I ran to the phone without reading the article and called my mother. When she answered, I said through my tears, "Is Jim dead? Is Jim dead?"

In a somber voice that I hadn't heard before, she said, "No, he's alive. He's hurt but he's alive. Come on home now."

When I got home, I found out what happened. My brother and three other Southern Miss students were driving home from Mardi Gras. Jim was driving. In the passenger seat was his date, a girl from Gulfport. In the backseat was one of Jim's best friends from Moss Point along with his date. A car driven by a drunk off-duty police officer from New Orleans crossed the median on Interstate 10 as they were leaving town. The cars hit head on. The two girls were killed instantly. Jim and his friend both sustained serious injuries and had to spend weeks in the hospital. They both eventually made a full recovery.

The days after the crash were surreal. We were thankful Jim was alive, but two girls whose lives were just beginning were dead. At one point, when the news was just getting back to Hattiesburg, Dad thought Jim had died also. Dad first heard of the accident when he got a call from the Kappa Alpha fraternity house where Jim lived. A fellow fraternity member was calling to see if my dad had heard the news. As he began to talk, Dad overheard somebody in the background say that Jim was dead and his friend was seriously injured. Hours went by before he found out Jim was alive. The news wouldn't be so good for the two girls' families. One of the girls' parents came by our house a few days after the accident. They sat and talked quietly with my parents in the living room. I didn't know what they were saying, but I did know there was a sadness in that house that I had never experienced before.

CHAPTER 6

McCool, You Stink!

As the sixth grade began, my brother's football career was over, but mine was just getting started. We had a new coach and we were going to be good. Jerry Spillman had been the coach at Mary Bethune, an elementary school on the other side of Hattiesburg. They hadn't lost a game in two years. He was our coach now, and we were going to find out what that felt like. We not only won every game but nobody scored against us and we never had to punt. Most of the players on that team were the same ones that only won two games the year before. Some people just know how to lead, and Coach Spillman was one of those people. He was the type of guy who would encourage you too. I used to catch a ride home with him after practice because my house was on his way. The last time he gave me a ride, he turned to me as I was getting out of the car.

He said, "Good luck to you. I got a feeling you're gonna go places."

"Thanks, Coach. Good luck to you too," I replied as I got out.

Just before he pulled off, he rolled the window down and said, "Oh, don't go breaking any more windows."

I smiled and waved and said, "I won't, Coach, I promise."

I didn't break any more windows, at least not in the sixth grade. I did everything right that year. I was appointed captain of the school safety patrol, which meant I was in charge of the crosswalks at the four street corners surrounding Thames elementary. I had a cool helmet and vest as proof of my authority over those crosswalks. Not one kid got flattened on his way to school that year, and I got a badge for it. Actually, there had never been a year where somebody had gotten flattened on their way to Thames elementary, but if they wanted to give me credit for 1972, I was taking it.

I got to play basketball for the first time that year too. Our team was good. I was not. I could dribble and shoot, but I never got the concept of running plays in basketball. It made sense in football. One guy takes the ball from one guy and gives it to another guy. Three guys run in front of him to block the guys trying to tackle him. That's a pretty simple concept to grasp. We're working together to get the ball in the end zone. I didn't see a need for that in basketball when all they had to do was pass it to me and let me fling it toward the basket. That's what I did too. It didn't matter where on the court I got the ball, I was jacking it up. Top of the key, twenty feet in the corner, fifteen-foot sky hook. I didn't care, if I got my hands on it, I was going up with it. My coach pulled me off the court one time and motioned for me to come sit beside him. I'm thinking he's going to give me pointers on better ways to get open.

He leaned over and said, "McCool, you stink! Now go sit on the end of the bench." I didn't play again the rest of the year, but we did win the city championship.

My basketball career might have been over, but I still had football. That was my ticket to stardom anyway. At least I thought it was until I got a dose of reality I probably could have done without. I was telling my brother, Jim, how I was going to be a pro football player.

He shook his head and said, "No, you're not, you're not good enough. Only the best player on each team moves up, and you're not even the best player on your team." Well gee, thanks for the encouragement. He was right of course. I was on my way to being a five nine white guy who could be timed in the forty-yard dash with an hour glass. Still, a little "Hey, give it all you got and see what happens" might have been more helpful.

Now my basketball coach had told me I stunk and god (my brother Jim) had told me I had no prayer at a career in football. Although, there was something coming up that I would eventually find out I had a knack for, entertainment. An end-of-year talent show was being held, and I jumped all over it. I just had to figure out what my talent was going to be. After crashing and burning with Pat McCool and the Harleys, there was no way this was going to be a musical act. So I decided to write, produce, and star in my very own skit. It was going to be a Western so I could wear a cowboy hat and a cool-looking holster with a set of six shooters. I signed up and got about the business of assembling a cast. We rehearsed all week, and the show was on Friday.

Everything started great. My actors were nailing their lines, and I was channeling Clint Eastwood. I was gaining confidence by the second as we headed to the great crescendo where I collar the bad guy. I was feeling so good as I delivered my last line that I decided to improvise. I was supposed to point my gun at Joey Helton who was lying on the ground with my foot on his neck and say, "Don't move or I'll blow the heck out of you." For some reason, I thought it would have more dramatic effect if I replaced the word heck with crap. It did! The word *crap* may seem less offensive to anyone reading this now, but this was 1972. As the word came out of my mouth, Joey Helton's eyes got as big as saucers and a loud gasp filled the auditorium. You would have thought I had mooned the entire audience. Realizing my gamble had not paid off, I did what I typically did when I sensed trouble. I took off running, out of the auditorium, down the hill behind the school, across the footbridge that led to my street and into my house.

I was shocked when my dad got home because he didn't say a word about it. I actually think he thought it was funny. My dad spent twenty-two years in the military and had been in two wars. I don't think he thought his son saying crap was some earth-shattering event. Surprisingly, I don't think the principal did either, but he had to say something to appease the mortified parents of the other students. First thing on Monday morning, after the roll was taken, the loud speaker cracked.

"Would Pat McCool please come to the office?"

I took one of those last mile strolls to the office knowing I was about to get a beating. My principal, Mr. Carol Russel, had no hesitation in giving me a beating whenever I had it coming. This was not one of those times. He calmly gave me one of those "This is why we can't have nice things" speeches and said, "I'll see you in July."

Mr. Russel was good friends with Dad, and they were both members of the Hattiesburg Civitan Club. Their main fundraiser was selling Cokes at the New Orleans Saints preseason practice held on Southern Miss's campus. The men of the club would sit across the street in the shade at the Coke stand, while I spent hours risking heat stroke walking around the practice field selling Cokes. I don't know if that's why he decided to pardon me, but the only thing I walked out of Mr. Russel's office with was a lifetime ban from ever stepping foot on that stage again.

A few days later, my class took an end-of-year field trip to Kamper Park. I was sitting next to Van on the miniature train that ran around the park. We were in the middle of the train. My basketball coach, the one that informed me that I had a remarkable lack of talent, was sitting in the front. A kid behind us picked up a rock and hurled it toward the coach. He looked around, and the first people he saw were the usual suspects, me and Van. So he fingered us as the rock hurlers. The fact that he didn't see us do it, because we didn't, was of little consequence. It was the type of thing that we would do, so we were convicted on the spot.

The next morning was the happiest day of the year, the final day of school. I bounced into my homeroom and took my seat. Just a few more hours and the prison gates would open and I would be furloughed for three solid months. My teacher started calling off names for roll call. She got to me and said, "Pat McCool." I threw my hand in the air and said, "Here today, gone tomorrow." The class erupted in laughter, and I was beaming. Then, the familiar sound cracked through the loudspeaker.

"Would Pat McCool and Van Overstreet please come to the principal's office?"

Wait a minute, what could I have possibly done this time? Every time I heard that in the past I had known exactly what I was being hauled in for, but this wasn't the past. This was 1972, and other than offending a bunch of self-righteous parents at the talent show, I had been squeaky clean. Not to mention I had been personally responsible for every kid in the Hillendale neighborhood of Hattiesburg, making it to and from school without being crushed by a car.

We walked to the principal's office, and my basketball coach was sitting in a chair talking to the principal. Mr. Russel looked up and said, "Fellows, Coach says you threw a rock at him yesterday. Is that true?"

"No, sir! No, sir, we didn't! I think it was some kid behind us, but it wasn't us!" I exclaimed.

"I saw you do it, McCool, both of you," the coach said.

At first I'm thinking, that doesn't make any sense, how do two people throw one rock? What really had me bewildered though was that an adult in a position of authority was blatantly lying. Of course, Mr. Russel had to side with the blatantly lying adult, so he made us stay after school as punishment. I was steamed. This was supposed to be the greatest day of the year. I was going to hear the final bell and bolt out of the back of the school while Richie Haven's Woodstock version of "Freedom" rang in my head. Now I had to stand at the exit door of the school for one hour after the bell rang and watch all my classmates stroll out and revel in the first moments of summer. To make matters worse, the blatantly lying coach who had caused this was going to stand with us so he could make sure we didn't say the heck with it and take off.

We were almost finished doing our time when Mrs. Bagsby walked by. Mrs. Bagsby was my favorite person at the school. She was in charge of safety and the one who had appointed me captain of the patrol. She believed in me and gave me a chance. I had come through with flying colors, until now. She asked the coach why we were having to stand there.

He said, "They acted up at the class picnic yesterday."

She gave me a concerned look and said, "Why, Pat? I am so disappointed in you." Then she turned and walked away. Just like that, my year of being an all-American boy had gone up in smoke.

The summer started, and baseball season was in full swing. I played third base for Standard Oil. I wasn't a huge fan of playing baseball, but I did like the cool uniforms and the chili dogs from the Frost Top that our coach would buy us after the games. I was a pretty good hitter up until the time Frank Odom nailed me in the head with a fastball. Frank was one of those kids who either had a massive growth spurt or his dad was lying about his age. He was four inches taller than everybody else and threw the ball hard. So hard you couldn't get out of the way if it was barreling toward you. It only took one of his fastballs off my skull to change my approach at the plate for good. I would stand at the back of the batter's box with one thing on my mind: not crawling back to the dugout with a knot on my head.

One day at practice, I was feeling tired in the ninety-five-degree Mississippi heat, so I leaned against the fence while we were shagging fly balls. My coach didn't appreciate my lack of enthusiasm, so he came over and let me know it. Dad came to pick me up from practice and offered to give two of my teammates that lived near us a ride home. On the way home, these two snitches decided to tell him about the behind chewing I had gotten by the coach. I wasn't thrilled that they did it, but I really didn't think much of it, until I got home. We walked in the house, and Dad grabbed me by the arm and angrily pulled me to his bedroom. He pulled out his belt and started wailing away on me. I tried to get away but that was met with an open hand to the head. It was the worst beating he had ever given me, and it was for not hustling at baseball practice. I didn't understand why I got that beating, but I did understand that I wasn't going to take another one.

CHAPTER 7

I THINK I WANT TO BE A
NARCOTICS OFFICER

The seventh grade started innocently enough, but it was going to go up in smoke too, a different kind of smoke. I played football in the fall and basketball in the winter. I was actually the starting power forward as the season began. That lasted ten minutes into the first game. We controlled the opening tip off, and our point guard dribbled toward the basket. He then passed the ball to me to initiate the play. I immediately shelved the game plan and hurled it toward the rim. I missed badly but I was undeterred. The next two times I touched the ball, I jacked it up and missed. Ten minutes into the game I was 0 for 3 and headed to the bench. A few days later, my friend and teammate Tracy English, who was a good basketball player, said the coach told him, "Pat ain't no basketball player." While this wasn't earth-shattering news, it was the second time I realized basketball coaches could be awfully judgmental.

As basketball season ended, I got another shot at acting and producing. My history teacher Mrs. Hosford, who would go down as my second favorite teacher of all time, decided we would do a historical Revolutionary War skit. She asked if anybody wanted to lead the production. Since I was the only one in the class with theatrical experience, I stepped forward. The skit would involve George Washington and Benedict Arnold. I, of course, chose myself to play George Washington. The script for the skit was already written. I decided this would be one of the few times I would learn from my mistakes, so I stuck to it. Other than a couple of flubbed lines by Benedict Arnold, the skit went great and Mrs. Hosford was proud. A few weeks later, she was giving a talk on leadership and used me as an example. She said "Like Pat, Pat is a leader. You saw how he took charge of the skit we did on George Washington." Words matter, and I never forgot those. They would come in handy years later.

Toward the end of the school year, a couple of Narcotics agents came to school to warn the student body of the evils of doing drugs. I listened intently as the officer told us how a college student had smoked marijuana and thought he could fly. So he jumped to his death off a five-story building. I thought preventing people from doing that would be a great way to spend my adult life, so I went home and told my brother Mike. We shared a room and would discuss all of the day's events as we fell asleep.

I said, "I think I'm gonna be a narcotics officer when I grow up."

Mike immediately leaned up in his bed with a "We need to talk" look on his face and said, "You know nobody likes narcs, right?" He then informed me of the reason for this. It was because narcs would arrest the cool kids who smoked pot, and he was in fact one of those cool kids. I thought my brother was one of the coolest guys on the planet and I wanted to be just like him. So I went from future DEA agent to wannabe pothead overnight.

The next day at school, I started talking to a friend of mine named "Randy." It turns out he had a cool older brother who smoked pot too. We decided that in order to reach our full coolness potential, we should become pot smokers ourselves. There was a guy my brother's age named "Bobby" who lived down the street from me. Bobby was a nice guy but a little awkward. He was overweight, had black horn-rimmed glasses, and a goofy looking Arlo Guthrie haircut. I figured anybody with an Arlo Guthrie haircut had to know where I could score some pot. Turns out I was right.

Bobby told me to give him five dollars for a matchbox and come by his house Friday after school. In the seventies, you generally bought pot two ways, fifteen dollars for a bag or five dollars for a matchbox. I gave him the five dollars and waited for Friday to arrive.

During class on Friday, Randy and I devised our game plan. I would pick up the matchbox after school, and Randy's older brother would drive him over to my house and pick me up. We would then drive around and smoke our first joint. I was excited. I went by Bobby's house after school and picked up the matchbox. He opened the front door of his house and tossed it to me. He then flashed me the peace sign and said, "Happy flying." I thought that was pretty cool and figured it must be how us pot smokers talked.

Randy and his brother picked me up, and we headed to the nearest country road. It doesn't take long to get to them in Hattiesburg, Mississippi. As soon as we got outside of the city limits, we pulled over so Randy's brother could roll a joint. When he opened the box, he said, "This smells funny, you sure this is real?" Well, there was only one way to find out and that was to smoke it. So we smoked the first joint and nothing happened. We then rolled and smoked another with the same result. We'd been had. It was oregano. Instead of smoking something smuggled in from Mexico, we were smoking something smuggled out of Bobby's mom's kitchen. We went back to Bobby's to get our money back, and he told me he had already spent it. Then Randy's brother who was bigger than Bobby went to the door and discovered that he actually hadn't spent it after all.

Every time I would hang out with Bobby throughout our teen years, we would always joke about that night. If Bobby was the one supplying the pot, we would joke, "Who brought the spaghetti to go with it?" The last time I saw Bobby, he seemed to have gotten his life together. He had lost weight, fixed his bowl cut, and graduated college. He also had a good job and had just gone out with one of the prettiest girls in town the night before. One week later, he shot and killed himself. That was the first time I realized that what you saw on the outside of a person didn't necessarily reflect what was going on inside of them.

Our next attempt to become potheads would not be as futile as the first. There was another kid named Bobby in the neighborhood who was known as the biggest pot smoker in town. I knew he could help me out. I was right. He sold me two joints for a buck each, and this time it wasn't a kitchen spice. Randy and I got my brother,

Mike, to drive us to the country club, and we smoked both of them along the way. The full effect didn't hit us until we got to the club and started playing ping pong. We started laughing hysterically and knocking ping pong balls all over the club house as the other kids watched in amusement. This went on for a couple of hours until the second phase of being stoned kicked in. We each then polished off about three chili cheeseburgers and a couple of orders of fries.

The seventh grade ended, and my dad forced me to play baseball. The season only lasted a few weeks for me because I took another fastball to the head. This one, right in my left eye socket. My eye swelled up so big I looked like Cyclops. I wasn't happy that I was going to spend the summer looking like a freak, but it did get me out of playing baseball. Now I could devote my time to my new passion, getting stoned.

Randy and I would get stoned and walk down to Burger Town, a popular local fast food place. Randy would order three hamburgers, eat the meat out of them, and throw the buns away. I didn't understand how he could afford to do that until he explained it to me. He was Jewish and over the age of thirteen. I was only twelve, but Randy had been held back a year in school so he was a year older. He explained that on his thirteenth birthday, his parents and all the adults at his synagogue had thrown him a party. At that party, they all gave him wads of cash totaling over $13,000. He pulled his bank book out and showed me the balance of $13,323. I was ready to convert on the spot. I would have even eaten that disgusting fish in the jar on the top shelf of his refrigerator.

The summer finally ended, and it was a good thing. If I had killed any more brain cells, I probably wouldn't have had enough to start the eighth grade. I was dreading it because I didn't want to play football, but my dad was going to make me. He made me and my brother play, and Mike was tired of it too. He actually swallowed half of a can of Skoal one day just to make himself sick so he wouldn't have to go to practice. I didn't want to just miss practice though, I wanted to miss the whole season. I was fresh off an early exit from baseball season because of an injury, so I thought that might be my ticket out of football. I just needed an injury debilitating enough to keep me from playing. So I devised a plan to dig a hole in the ground deep enough for my foot to go down to the ankle. I would get a running start, plant my foot in the hole, and twist my ankle as I ran through it. I don't remember if I chickened out or just wasn't stupid enough to go through with it, but I didn't.

Then I came up with plan B. I would just hang out at school until practice was over and then head home. I was developing a unique ability to not think things through, so Dad showing up at a game and noticing that I was not on the sideline hadn't occurred to me. As it turned out, I didn't have to worry about that, because on the first day of preseason practice, one of the coaches called and informed him that I was not on the field. He showed up at the school twenty minutes later. I was hanging out in the field house talking to the equipment manager, a friend of mine named Lanny. He burst through the door, slammed me against the wall, slapped me in the face and yelled, "You get your equipment on and get your butt out on that field." I did what he said, but I didn't like him anymore.

If my dad had known the fateful meeting that was about to take place on that field, he might not have sent me out there. We were running a drill where you would line up across from another player. The coach would blow the whistle, and both players would run together and start knocking the snot out of each other until one of you ended up on the ground. When it was my turn, I looked across the line to size up the guy who would be attempting to knock the snot out of me. He was a new kid at school I had never seen before. He was kind of skinny with blond curly hair hanging out of his helmet and was wearing white Adidas cleats with orange stripes. I was thinking that this was going to be easy. It wasn't. The coach blew the whistle, and we tangled up and went after it until he blew it again. Neither one of us ended up on the ground. We just stared at each other as we walked back to the other group of players. After practice, I walked up to him and shook his hand and asked him his name.

"Bryant O'Connell, what's yours?" he asked.

"Pat McCool, good job out there. I wasn't expecting you to put up that much of a fight," I replied.

He laughed and said, "Yeah, you too. I didn't think he was ever gonna blow that whistle."

Just like that, what my brother, Jim, would later call fire and dynamite had just come together. It would be a while before the explosion, but it was coming.

As the school year began, Randy and I had the opportunity to join the high school fraternity TEKE (Theta Kappa Omega). It was a social and philanthropic organization. That is if you call raising money for keg parties where each member would drink themselves silly, social and philanthropic. We actually weren't eligible to join until we were in the ninth grade, but my brother Mike was a member and all the other members knew me, so they let us in a year early. We went through our month long pledge period and took our fifty licks from the TEKE pledge paddle and we were one of the big boys.

The fundraiser for our first keg party was going to be a bake sale. Each member would bring a cake to Roses department store, and we would set up a table out front and sell them. Randy and I didn't know how to bake a cake, but we figured, how hard could it be? We scoured his mom's kitchen to see if she had any cake-baking materials. We found two boxes of cake mix and one can of chocolate icing. We mixed the cake mixes and realized we had a problem. His mother only had four cake pans, three round ones and a square one. We didn't have time to bake them separately so one of them wasn't going to look right. We figured cake was cake and who cared if the bottom was square as long as it tasted like cake. We finished baking the cakes and put the chocolate icing on the one with the square bottom. Then we realized we had another problem. Our initial plan was to spread the chocolate icing thinly on each cake so we would have enough for both of them. That didn't work, so we ended up with a chocolate cake with a square bottom and round cake with no icing. We went back to the pantry and started scouring some more. All we could find was an unopened jar of crunchy peanut butter. We were out of time and with no other option, so we started spreading. The crunchy peanut butter didn't stick to the cake like we thought it would, but we kept working until we got it covered.

We showed up to the bake sale and put them on the table, and the rest of the guys just shook their heads and laughed. At the end of the day, the only cakes that were left were our two masterpieces. My brother's friend, Charles Blackledge, decided to mark them down to one dollar each as a last-ditch effort to sell them. Surprisingly, a guy in a truck pulled up and bought the one with the square bottom. He said, "Heck yeah, I'll buy it. Cake's cake." Which is exactly what Randy and I had thought. The crunchy peanut butter cake ended up stuck on a Stop sign on Thirty-Fourth Avenue.

Our next fundraiser wouldn't be nearly as labor intensive but just as profitable. One of the leaders of the fraternity decided we would market something that would sell easily and wouldn't require us to stand in front of Roses department store for eight hours on a Saturday.

We were going to sell a pound of marijuana. In the early seventies, a pound of pot cost $140. If you broke it into sixteen one-ounce bags and sold them for $15 each (the going rate), that would be a $100 profit. That was more than enough to buy a keg of beer and have some breathing room to cover the couple of guys that would smoke the pot themselves and not pony up the cash.

The drug dealing scheme went off as planned, and only one guy smoked up part of the profit.

I got home over an hour late the night of the keg party, and my dad was waiting for me. He could tell I had been drinking and decided he was going give me a beating. I decided he wasn't. I jumped out of my bedroom window and sprinted down the street. This would happen about five more times until Dad realized that you couldn't hit a moving target. At first I would sleep in the woods on a bed of pine straw until I discovered that not all of the houses that were for sale in the neighborhood had locked doors. I would stay gone for days until Dad and Mike finally found me and brought me home.

By the time the school year was ending, Bryant O'Connell and I were becoming buddies. The last week of the year the school was holding their annual teacher-student basketball game with members of the faculty playing against members of the student body. Bryant and I decided that blowing up the backstop on the baseball field would be a great way to end the year with a bang. I had recently watched a movie where a Molotov cocktail had been used for a similar purpose, so that was our explosive of choice. I was to bring the two-liter Coke bottle full of gas, and he was supposed to bring the torn piece of bed sheet for the fuse. He brought a paper towel instead.

For any wannabe terrorist reading this, the reason you use a piece of cloth for a fuse is because it burns slowly. This gives you the opportunity to light the fuse, throw it at whatever you want to blow up, and high tail it out of harm's way before the fire starts. That's not what happened. I lit the paper towel, and it instantly ignited the gas in the bottle and almost burned both of us to a crisp. I dropped the flaming bottle on the ground, and we took off running. We didn't stop until we were about a mile away.

When we looked back, we could see a bright red glow. It looked like the whole school was on fire. Fortunately, it wasn't. The baseball field was a long way from the school. The reason the flames had gotten so bright was because the field was rarely used and weeds and straw had grown around the backstop. It just burned for about thirty minutes and went out. The next day, we showed up at school with singed hair and eyebrows so it was obvious who the pyromaniacs were. Surprisingly, we didn't get in any trouble. The only thing that was said was by a coach when I walked into gym class.

My football coach, Ed Soberieski, looked at me with a big smile and said, "Thanks, McCool, I appreciate you taking care of all those weeds around the baseball field, saved me a lot of work."

CHAPTER 8

WELL, MAYBE I WON'T BE A NARCOTICS OFFICER

Summer finally arrived, and I had a decision to make. Alcohol and pot weren't cheap, so I needed a way to make some money. One option was to go back to busing tables like I had done the year before at my friend's father's restaurant. I had no problem with busing tables except for the part where I had to show up and bus tables. I was also fresh off my lesson in capitalism given to me by my role models in my high school fraternity. I liked the idea of turning a profit without breaking a sweat. I could put in thirty hours washing dishes for one hundred dollars or I could sell sixteen bags of pot and take home the same amount. I decided to opt for the one that was less labor intensive. I figured the fact that it was illegal was only a minor detail. It wasn't. I got busted the first day on my new job.

It turns out that a telephone pole across the street from a neighbor's house was not the best place to stash my inventory while I went home to take a shower. As I rounded the corner, there were two narcotics officers waiting for me.

"Is this yours?" one officer asked.

"Nope, never seen it," I replied.

"Well, your neighbor saw you put it there," he said.

"Okay, it's mine," I confessed.

I went on to explain that I had found it in the woods and it was strictly for personal use. This might have been slightly plausible if there wasn't a scale and a box of Glad bags in the paper sack with the pound of pot. Unfortunately, there was, so at thirteen years old I was going down for possession of marijuana with intent to sell. News of this swept like wild fire throughout Hattiesburg, Mississippi. I went from that mischievous McCool kid to head of the Hattiesburg chapter of the Gambino crime family overnight. I never actually became a teenage drug dealer, but it didn't matter. I had earned the reputation of being one, and it would stay with me for a long time.

I got one year of juvenile probation and the threat of going to Columbia Training school for boys. I was very fortunate. This was the mid-seventies in Mississippi. There were adults in the state penitentiary for having a couple of joints. Most kids would have gotten free room and board at that training facility for what I had been caught with. Luckily for me, I wasn't most kids. I was the son of Lieutenant Colonel James Max McCool. Everybody in town respected the "the Colonel," which made me a bad kid from a "good" family. So I got off with probation. It may have been better if I hadn't, but I did, and it would happen over and over again.

I managed to go through the rest of the summer without getting caught doing anything wrong. My drug-dealing days (or day) were behind me, but my pot-smoking days weren't. The average summer night for me and my friends would start at the Minit Mart on Twenty-Eighth Avenue across from Forrest General Hospital. This was the Minit Mart that Jimmy Buffet sang about stealing from in his song "Peanut Butter Conspiracy" during his days as a student at Southern Miss. We would load ice chests with beer or the cheapest bottle of bourbon we could afford and a two-liter Coke and cruise the back roads of Forrest and Lamar County until we had smoked all our pot. We would then head back into town and begin an intense search for carnal knowledge of the opposite sex.

The biggest threat of getting into trouble was having a police car get behind your car. The moment the driver of the car saw the police in his rearview mirror, he would make the mistake of informing his passengers by saying, "Whatever you do, do not turn around. There's a cop behind us." Of course that is exactly what everybody did. Nothing tells a police officer that you're up to no good like five wide-eyed teenagers with long hair staring out of the back window. Fortunately for me, that didn't happen the rest of the summer and I was on to the ninth grade.

CHAPTER 9

FIRE AND DYNAMITE

I was playing football again but not because dad was making me. I wanted to play. I liked playing football. I just didn't like being forced to play. I also had a reputation to live down, and this could only help. On the first day of practice, I was walking onto the practice field and heard someone walking up behind me. It was our defensive coordinator, "Coach Stead."

As he approached me, he said, "Hey, McCool, I've heard a lot about you."

I'm thinking, "Well this is just great, I'm gonna get kicked off the team before they blow the first whistle." That is not what happened. He proceeded to tell me that he knew some guys who knew me and that he could trust me and I could trust him. I had no idea what him trusting me and me trusting him meant. He then leaned closer and whispered, "I want to see if you can hook me up with some joints." I stood there in silent disbelief for a moment. Then it starts to dawn on me. He's not kicking me off the team because he thinks I'm a drug dealer. He wants me to become *his* drug dealer.

Now I wasn't the sharpest knife in the drawer, but I was smart enough to know that immediately agreeing to bring pot to my football coach might not be a good idea. I said I might could help him out, and he said we could work out a deal. Now I'm curious to know what kind of deal he's talking about. Was he talking about cutting me some slack in practice? The other players and coaches would surely notice if he let me out of Oklahoma drills and belly flops. No, the stakes were bigger than that. As it turned out, he was also my science teacher. He said if I would give him a bag of pot each semester, he would give me a passing grade.

Okay, now we're communicating. I told him I needed to enlist the help of a friend, but it looks like we can do business. I couldn't afford fifteen dollars a semester for a bag of pot, so I asked Bryant, also in the science class if he wanted to go in with me. He was all over it. We saved our lunch money over the next week and bought the bag of pot. We pulled a little out for ourselves before we gave it to him. After all, he was getting it for free, so he shouldn't complain. He didn't. The semester ended, and the only work Bryant and I had done was sign our names to the tests and hand them in. The report cards finally came out, and there it was, a shiny B standing out in a sea of Ds and C minuses.

Bryant and I got in minor trouble throughout the rest of the first half of the year. Our parents didn't come down too hard on us because we were pulling Bs in science. Maybe they thought we were just idiot savants that were bored with the other stuff but had a future in science.

The Christmas holidays came and we had two weeks of free time on our hands so we needed some cash. We decided to try our hand at petty theft. Petty theft wasn't actually the plan, but as is the case with most criminal enterprises concocted by knuckleheads, that's what it turned out to be.

I had been in the convenience store at closing time on Lincoln road a week earlier. I was trying to decide between the bean and cheese burrito and a box of honey buns when the store clerk started turning the lights off. I made my choice and headed to the counter before he locked the door. He rang me up and said, "I almost locked you in." The light bulb immediately started flashing in my head. What if he had locked me in? I would have had total run of the place. I could have gotten the burrito, honey bun, and all the squirt cheese I could eat before I made my way to the cash register.

Bryant, as usual, thought it was a brilliant plan. We hung around outside of the store a few minutes before closing time. We waited for a few people to walk in and distract the clerk so we wouldn't be noticed. When the time was right, we slipped in undetected, or so we thought. The clerk turned out the lights and locked up while we huddled together on the canned goods aisle. Just like that, the place was ours for the taking. We then did the last thing a hardened criminal should do when committing a crime, start worrying about getting caught. Panic set in, so we ran to the cash register. It was locked. We then tried the door under the register and found a bag of rolled coins. Right at that moment, a car pulled into the parking lot. We thought it was a cop and we were moments away from being surrounded. We each grabbed a carton of cigarettes and headed out of the back door with the bag of coins. We slid down into the creek behind the store and sprinted to freedom. We got to Bryant's house and sized up our take. We had only gotten away with two cartons of Vantage cigarettes and seventeen dollars in coins, not even a can of Spam to celebrate. At least we had gotten away.

The next day, we were at Bryant's house and heard a knock at the door. It was two police officers. They wanted to talk to us about the burglary at the convenience store. A kid from the neighborhood had seen us go in and not come out. I confessed on the spot. That was becoming my MO when facing insurmountable evidence. Confess immediately, burst into tears, and throw myself on the mercy of the authorities while proclaiming how incredibly remorseful I was. This went well with the "wayward kid from a good family who had made a bad decision" narrative that had served me well to that point. It worked again, and we got some psychological counseling and went back to school to begin the new year.

Everything was going smoothly until about six weeks into the year. My brother, Mike, drove me to school one day, and coach Stead was standing in the parking lot. He approached the car as we pulled up and I rolled down the window.

He said, "Hey, I just wanted to tell you that I'm going to be doing a new gig and everything's going to be cool."

I had no idea what he was talking about. I said, "Yeah okay, Coach, see ya in class," and Mike pulled to the front of the school.

Four hours later, I found out what he was talking about. Bryant and I walked into science class and took our seat. As we settled into our seats, we noticed a small Asian woman walk in and sit at coach Stead's desk. I asked the guy beside me where Coach Stead was. He lived in the same part of town as Coach Stead, so I figured he would know. He said Coach Stead had been fired. Turns out he had forged his teaching certificate. While I felt bad for Coach Stead, I felt worse for me and Bryant. We had been riding those Bs all year and we were in desperate need of another one. We weren't going to get it. That day was test day, and it was being given by the Asian lady who hadn't cracked a smile since she entered the room.

She passed out the tests, and Bryant and I just looked at each other. We were doomed. We hadn't opened a book all year, and the only question on that test that we knew the answer to was our name. We decided we wouldn't turn ours in. Maybe she wouldn't notice. Toward the end of class, we were sitting on the counter by the windows talking to Van. We explained our predicament, and he started laughing. He then pointed to a stack of papers sitting beside him.

He said, "Those are the tests."

I don't know why the new teacher thought it would be a good idea to leave them there but she did. He then thumbed through the tests, pulled his out, tossed a lighter on top of them, and pushed the stack towards me. I knew what he was suggesting. If those tests went up in flames, so would the evidence that Bryant and I hadn't turned ours in. I know that doesn't sound logical, but we weren't relying on logic for our decisions, so we lit them on fire and tossed them out of the window. We assumed they would just fall to the ground and quietly burn. As usual, we assumed wrong. They landed on a row of dried weeds and burst into flames similar to what happened with our first attempt at arson. Fortunately, the bell rang, so we bolted out of the class and didn't stop running until we got to the gym for our final period. As soon as the bell stopped ringing, the loudspeaker cracked with a familiar sound. "Would Pat McCool and Bryant O'Connell please come to the office and bring your books. We weren't surprised about being summoned to the office, but why did we have to bring our books?

The principal at Lillie Burney Junior High School was Mrs. Clara Weathersby AKA the Hawk. It was a name she came by honestly. She didn't suffer fools lightly, and we were two fools that she would no longer suffer at all. She stepped out of her office, pointed at two chairs and said, "Sit right there until your parents get here."

Oh no, this sounded serious. Why were our parents coming, and why did we have our books? It was because she was kicking us out of Lillie Burney and refusing to let us come back. This was not good because Lillie Burney was the only ninth grade in the Hattiesburg public school system.

Our only other option was Beeson Academy. It was the private school some of the kids in the neighborhood attended. Somehow our fathers got the school board at Beeson to accept us, so we enrolled the following week. This could have been a great opportunity for us because some of the coolest guys in town went there, and more importantly some of the prettiest girls. On the first day of school while we were sitting in the gym, two of those prettiest girls came up and introduced themselves. If these two girls were introducing themselves, it meant we had a chance to fit in and thrive in our new environment. All we had to do was refrain from doing something stupid and we were on our way. Of course that was impossible and we were about to take stupid to a whole new level.

On the third day at our new school, Bryant showed up stressed out over a falling out he had with his dad the night before. I don't know what this had to do with me, but I was down for whatever rebellion he had in mind. Bryant had a few hundred dollars he had saved up from a part-time job and suggested we go to New Orleans to see Kiss who was playing during Mardi Gras. Seemed like a swell idea to me, after all, we were already fourteen and hadn't even been to Mardi Gras. We spent about two minutes devising our plan of action, then the bell rang. We walked out of the school and down the driveway, tossing our books in a puddle of water along the way. We had to get to Bryant's house to get his money, but I had business I wanted to take care of first. I was convinced my old friend Randy had stolen a sizable amount of pot from my brother, Mike (because he had) but I got blamed for it. This had been burning inside me for months, and I figured since we were leaving town for good this would be a great time to settle the score.

We walked out onto the road in front of the school and started hitch hiking toward Lillie Burney where Randy was in class. A girl from Beeson pulled out of the school a minute later and offered us a ride. We got to the school and put our plan in motion. We would walk into Randy's class, and Bryant would stand at the door and watch the hallway while I gave Randy the business for betraying our friendship. As I stepped into the classroom, I dropped a lit cigarette in the trash can and right on cue it caught fire. I don't know what it was about me and fire but whatever I put a light to would instantly burst into flames. Well, the teacher started screaming as the fire shot out of the trash can and we hadn't planned for that, so we took off running.

A couple of hours later, we made it back to our neighborhood where we would spend the night before we headed off to start our new lives. We knew the police were searching for us all over town, so we had to keep a low profile. We ran into a friend of ours named Larry who had an attic on top of his garage, and he let us sleep there for the night. The next day, we walked to the Richburg Road overpass at Interstate 59, which was about ninety miles north of New Orleans. We stuck our thumbs out and started walking south. A few minutes later, a car with three college guys on their way to Mardi Gras stopped and gave us a ride to the French Quarter. Our first stop was the place that sold fake IDs because as fugitives we felt like we needed a new identity. That new identity also made us four years older. We were fourteen years old and looked every bit of it but that didn't matter. We were now adults and had the Louisiana driver's licenses to prove it.

Our next order of business was to find a strip club. We had heard about them for years and now was the time to see what all the fuss was about. We headed for Bourbon Street and didn't have to go any further. Every other business was a strip club. We stopped at the first one and just stood on the sidewalk leering in like a couple of peeping toms. While we were debating whether or not to go in, we were approached by an older guy named "Mattie." He asked us what we were up to, and we explained we were trying to decide if we wanted to go inside the club. He suggested we didn't. He said the girls in there just wanted to take money from suckers and we shouldn't waste ours. This was great. This guy was giving us solid street advice that we needed. He asked us where we were staying, and since we now knew we could trust him, we explained our situation. For some reason, he wasn't surprised. He said we could stay with him for twenty dollars a week until we found a place. Just like that, we had a place to stay and a cool guy willing to teach us the ropes.

We hopped into his new Trans Am and rode over the River Bridge to his apartment on the West Bank. He had a cool apartment with a lava lamp. We had never seen one before and we just sat there staring at it. Then he asked us where we were from and we told him. He pulled out a photo album and started turning through it and finally stopped on a page and showed it to us.

"You know these guys?" he asked as he showed us two pictures. They were pictures of two of my brother Mike's friends. It was two guys who both had reputations for getting into trouble just like me and Bryant, so naturally we looked up to them. If they were friends with Mattie, he must be on the up and up.

About this time, a guy walked in who looked just like Bob Seger. He seemed like a really cool guy and he was from Detroit, so I thought he and "Bob" might be related. They weren't, but he seemed like a nice enough guy and we sat around smoking pot and drinking beer until Mattie decided to go to bed. That's when things stopped being so cool. Mattie asked me and Bryant which one of us wanted to sleep in the room with him. Uh, I don't know Mattie. I think the answer to that is going to be neither of us. He asked if we were sure, like we weren't answering the question right, but we assured him we would be just fine right there on the couch. He finally went to bed, and "Bob Seger" looked at us and laughed. He explained what Mattie had in mind and that he wasn't just being a cool guy. He said if we were freaked out about it, he was going to Los Angeles the next day and if we wanted, we could go with him. We were and we did. How hard could it be to go to LA? We didn't have to pack because we were wearing everything we owned. So we fell asleep sitting on the couch with plans to head to LA the next day.

The next day, we went down and waited in front of the apartment for the guy who was going to drive us to Los Angeles. After waiting about thirty minutes, I asked Bob Seger if he thought the guy was coming. He said, "I don't know. I just met him last night." Well, that's comforting. The guy we met the night before was waiting on the guy he met the night before to drive us to LA. What could go wrong here? A few minutes later, our guy pulled up. He looked more like Charles Manson without the beard than a rock star, but we piled in anyway.

We start driving west on Interstate 10 toward Texas. Bob Seger and the driver were talking, but Bryant and I weren't really paying attention. I think we were more focused on the fact that every mile we drove was one mile farther away from home than we had ever been without our parents. We did tune in to the conversation when we heard Bob Seger ask the driver if he had a gun. The guy said he did. He reached in the glove compartment and pulled out a large caliber pistol. I didn't know why this guy had a gun, but I did know that I didn't want to see him use it.

We got to Houston in the afternoon and pulled into the bus station. They're going to show us how to make a few bucks the easy way. The plan, they explained, was to buy a locker key for a couple of dollars then watch for somebody who looked like they had some money or valuables approach a locker. As they start to put their luggage in the locker, step up and offer to help. When you had finished helping them, you would switch keys and give them yours. When they left, you could steal all their belongings. Seemed like a great life skill to have, but one Bryant and I had no plans to use. Fortunately, nobody showed up who looked as if they had anything worth stealing, so the guys eventually decided to leave.

As we left the bus station, we were apparently in such a hurry to reach California that the driver couldn't wait for the red light to turn green. As he drove through it, a car slammed into the side of ours, knocking us across the intersection. It was a big collision, but the car we were in didn't sustain much damage. The other car was a smoking heap stuck in the middle of the intersection. An elderly woman got out of the car and seemed quite distressed, so we started to get out to see if she was okay. Our driver told us to get back in the car and he would handle it. We got back in the car and watched as he talked to her for about a minute. He then quickly walked back to the car, jumped in, and drove off. As we drove off, I watched the woman screaming and crying in the middle of the intersection. Our plan was beginning to take a bad turn, but really we had no plan.

We drove for hours into the Texas night, eventually pulling into the small town of Columbus, Texas. We stopped at a convenience store to pick up a case of Lone Star beer. Then we checked into a cheap hotel and started drinking. As the alcohol started to kick in, Bryant, for some inexplicable reason, started telling these guys how tough we were. He told them about all the guys we had beaten up in Mississippi. This was news to me. I think the closest either one of us had gotten to a fight was the occasional bro off, which ended with no punches being thrown. Regardless of the truth, he was laying it on pretty heavy. He even went so far as to tell them we had cut some kid's fingers off. I had no idea where this was coming from, but all I was thinking was, "Hey, speak for yourself." I didn't want to give them the slightest reason to think I wanted to fight anybody. Especially either one of them. Bryant, on the other hand, was doubling down and challenged Bob Seger. This ended quickly. The driver stood up and dropped Bryant with one punch to the stomach. Bryant let out a groan and fell onto the bed and passed out. This was starting to get scary, but I was drunk and had no place to go, so I drifted off to sleep and hoped for the best.

A little while later, Bob Seger woke me up and said, "Look, you seem like you're okay, but we don't like your friend."

"You can go with us, but we ain't taking him." I told him thanks, but I was staying with Bryant and fell back asleep.

The next day, we both woke up with massive hangovers. Our buddies were gone, and so was our money. We're now stuck somewhere in the middle of Texas with no money and no way home. We came to the realization that a beating from our fathers wasn't nearly as bad as a beating from a pistol packing guy who left crying old ladies in the middle of the street. We had two choices. We could wave the white flag and call home for somebody to come get us, or we could steal a car and drive home ourselves. Since this journey started with a monumentally bad decision, it only seemed to reason that we would end it with one. We decided to steal a car, never mind the fact that neither one of us knew how to drive.

I decided I would go find our transportation home while Bryant waited in the hotel. We figured one scruffy-looking guy walking the streets of Columbus, Texas would look less conspicuous than two, so off I went. There was a Dairy Queen about one hundred yards from the hotel, so I decided to try there first. There were people eating underneath an outdoor canopy attached to the restaurant, so I walked around to the back. There was a car parked by the back door. It was a brand-new green Oldsmobile Cordoba with a white landau top. I walked by the driver's side door to see if the keys were in it. They were. There was just a screen door between the car and the inside of the restaurant. The people inside could see the car, so I'm sure they had no reason to fear leaving the keys in the ignition. Besides, this was 1975 in Columbus, and no one had to worry about having their car stolen. Until now.

I circled back around the car and jumped in. I fired it up and hit the gas. This was the first time I had ever even been behind the wheel of a car, so I was having to figure it out on the fly. The parking lot of the Dairy Queen was made of gravel, so the car started fish tailing as I rounded the corner. I can still remember the frightened looks on the faces of the people eating under the canopy as the front of that car pointed towards them with gravel flying out from the back wheels. This could have ended very badly, but it didn't. Somehow that car straightened up and I gained control and pulled out onto the road. I turned into the hotel parking lot and honked the horn for Bryant. He came running out of the room with two pillows in his arms. I was puzzled by the pillows. We had put no thought into anything we had done during this entire ordeal, but now he's thinking about our comfort on the trip home.

It turned out we didn't need the pillows after all, because as soon as we pulled onto Interstate 10, a car topped the hill behind us at a high rate of speed. It was two Texas Rangers, and they did not have a cheery disposition. They quickly pulled beside us, and the one in the passenger seat leaned out and pointed a .44 Magnum directly at my head. He was shaking his head back and forth in a way that indicated to me that I had about five seconds to pull that car over. I did, and by the time the car stopped they were already opening our doors and yanking us out. They slammed both of us onto the hood of the car, cuffed our hands behind our backs, and hauled us to the local jail. When we got there, we found out why they may have been a little more upset than usual. The car we had stolen belonged to the sister of the local judge.

For some reason, we never had to meet that judge. They just threw us in a cell together and slammed the door. Nobody said anything to us the whole time we were there. I guess because we were fourteen they were just waiting for somebody to come pick us up and take us back to Mississippi. We were in a cell at the top of a flight of stairs separated from the other inmates. We couldn't see them but we could hear them and what we heard made us glad we couldn't. The guard would bring us a bowl of oatmeal in the morning and two bologna sandwiches in the afternoon. If there was anything positive from this whole fiasco, it was learning how good Thousand Island dressing tasted on a bologna sandwich. A couple of days passed and we hadn't heard anything from anybody. We had no idea what was going to happen next or how long we would be there. Seconds felt like minutes and minutes felt like hours. We found a deck of cards and would play a game where we would see who could throw the most cards into one of our oatmeal bowls but that got old quick.

On the third day, Bryant lay down on the cot I had been sleeping on. He had noticed me carve something on the metal beside the cot and wanted to see what it was. It was the name Kim. She was my on-again, off-again girlfriend. It was on and off because it was on when she decided it was on and off when she decided it was off. She liked me some of the time and some of the time she didn't. Our relationship was also hindered by the fact that her parents strictly forbid her to be anywhere near me. She also liked Bryant, maybe even more than me, but I had kept Bryant from liking her. I badmouthed her to him every chance I got. All the usual things. She's goofy, she's skinny, she's stupid, I would be embarrassed to be seen with her, and he bought every bit of it. The truth was, if she would have liked me as much as I liked her, I would have told Bryant to go pound sand

and spent all my time with her. The second he saw that I had carved her name on the wall, he knew that. We went from partners in crime to enemies in an instant and we were locked together in a ten-by-ten foot cell.

Fortunately, the next morning, the guard came and opened the cell. Unfortunately, he was coming for Bryant not me. Bryant's dad had a friend in Texas with a plane and he was flying Bryant home. I had no idea at the time where he had gone. The guard opened the door and told Bryant to come with him and that was the last I would see of him for a while. It would be three more days before the guard came for me. My dad was waiting outside to drive me home.

I had never been so happy to see my dad. I didn't care if he gave me an epic pounding right there in the parking lot of the jail. I deserved it, and I wouldn't have complained a bit. I couldn't believe I was walking out of that jail and going home. When I found out I wasn't going to have to come back and pay for what I had done, I was even more ecstatic. They were done with me and I was done with them. The ride home was quiet. Surprisingly, Dad didn't get on to me on the long ride home. I could tell he was disgusted with me and simmering on the inside, but I think he was just happy to have me back alive. He told me how worried my mother had been because she had no idea if she would ever see me again. He let that sink in as we drove through East Texas.

When I got back, I found out that the state of Mississippi had nothing to say about what happened in Texas and running away from home wasn't actually a crime. My only punishment was being grounded until further notice, which lasted about two weeks. I got more good news when I discovered I didn't have to finish the ninth grade. For some reason, they were going to just move me right on to the tenth. It was probably because the ninth grade principal, Clara "the hawk" Weathersby wouldn't allow me back on the property. Whatever the reason, they weren't getting any argument from me. I was more than happy to lay around the house and watch game shows and soap operas until summer came. What I wasn't happy about was Bryant had come home and stolen my girlfriend. The next meeting between Bryant and me wouldn't be nearly as pleasant as the first one.

CHAPTER 10

ONE CERTAIN SUMMER

Summer arrived, and I was a couple of months away from getting my driver's license. My routine was set. I would go down to the Minit Mart in the early evening and hop up on my perch between two newspaper racks in front of the store, the *Hattiesburg American* on the right and *The Clarion-Ledger* on the left. It was like my own personal throne. I would sit there until the crowd started showing up. I would get in the car with somebody who had the same agenda as me, and we would head off for a night of drinking and debauchery. Most of the people I was hanging with were older than me. I was still only fourteen and didn't have a car. I needed a car for the activities in which I was participating. I mean you couldn't go over to your fourteen year old friend's house and smoke pot and drink whiskey. Not to mention that picking up girls while walking was virtually impossible. Besides that, there weren't many fourteen-year-old kids left in my part of town whose parents would let them have anything to do with me.

One of the older guys I hung with the most was Charles Blackledge. Charles was like a brother to me. He had actually been the best friend of my brother Mike's for years until Mike met his girlfriend and started spending all his time with her. On more than one occasion when I was younger, if someone older gave me trouble, Mike and Charles would pay them a visit. Charles was a good guy too. He drank and smoked with the best of them but was respectful to adults and would always do the right thing.

One night, Charles and I had too much to drink. Well, just about every night we had too much to drink, but this night we flattened a neighbor's mailbox with Charles's car. He showed up at my house at seven o'clock the next morning and said, "Let's go."

"Go where?" I asked.

"We gotta go fix that mailbox." I didn't even remember hitting a mailbox, and I sure as heck wouldn't have been going to fix it if the person who owned it didn't see me do it. We went and bought a brand-new mailbox better than the one that was there and lost about five pounds of fluid each sweating in the Mississippi heat until we got it put up. The owner of the house saw us and walked out to see what we were doing.

Charles said, "Uh, yes, sir. I'm sorry but we had a flat tire on the way home last night and it caused us to run over your mailbox, so we're here to fix it." We had actually gotten the flat tire when we crashed into the mailbox. However it happened, the guy was happy with his new one.

It was going to be an *American Graffiti* kind of night. Friendships would be renewed, scores would be settled, and lives would be changed. It started out innocently enough. I walked down to the Minit Mart and took my place on the newspaper racks like I had done every day for the first half of the summer. A few minutes later, the crowd started showing up. Charles pulled in the parking lot in his silver Chevy Vega. Chevy Vegas were cool little cars but they were probably the biggest pieces of junk that Chevrolet ever made. You won't see any of them on the road today because once they broke down they were too expensive to fix. Charles's was still in good shape, and we would be rolling in it that night.

The first place we would be rolling to was Reed Green Coliseum. I've had some of my fondest moments at Reed Green. I've watched great victories by the Southern Miss basketball team and seen top acts from Bob Dylan to Bob Hope. The night I saw Bob Hope wasn't one of my fondest moments. It's not that I didn't like Bob Hope. I was a big fan of Bob Hope as a kid and happy to go see him. I just wasn't happy to be wearing the blue seersucker suit and shiny white dress shoes my mother made me wear. To make matters worse, halfway through the show, my mother and grandmother tried to molest Bob in front of God and everybody. He had a habit of walking through the crowd while he sang. I'm sure it had worked well everywhere else he had done it, but he couldn't have been prepared for what happened when he walked past Sally and Polly McCool. They jumped out of their seats and wrapped their arms around his waist and legs and gave him a bear hug. Fortunately for me, I had been so humiliated by the outfit from Sears my mother had made me wear that I was hiding at the top of the stairs and didn't have to be associated with them.

There would be no humiliating moments tonight. The Band was coming to town. I had never heard of them, but Charles said they used to play with Bob Dylan and that was good enough for me. Before we left for the concert, we hung around to see what would be happening after it ended. The usual suspects showed up, and we found out there would be a party at Greg Shanklin's house later that night.

As we were getting ready to leave, I noticed a couple pull up in a yellow Ford Pinto with a black stripe on the side. It was a guy named Robert Spade and his girlfriend, Polly. He was tall with shoulder-length blond hair, and she was a pretty girl with long black hair. I didn't actually know either one of them. I just knew who they were from the neighborhood. I always admired them because they seemed to be content to just spend time with each other. They would stop by the Minit Mart, chat for a few minutes, and drive off together. That's what they did that night. They backed out of the parking lot, waved to everybody, and drove off down Twenty-Eighth Avenue.

Charles and I drove over to the coliseum. We parked the car and headed for the fence. Most people went through the ticket gate, but that wasn't how we accessed the interior of Reed Green. The ticket gates at Reed Green were located at the barbed wire fence that surrounded the coliseum. Once you got through them, you could then just walk inside the building. There were three sets of doors to the building. Only two of the sets of doors had working ticket booths. One was left unattended. If you could get over the fence at that location, you could stroll right in. If you tried to climb the fence, you would tear yourself to shreds on the barbed wire on top, unless you first crawled up onto the concrete wall to which it was attached. The fence that crossed that wall was only three feet high but there was a twenty-foot drop off on the other side. If you could avoid falling off the wall and breaking your neck, you could step right over and walk in, which is exactly what we did every time there was a concert at Reed Green Coliseum. The Band was awesome. I had never seen them before, but once I heard Levon Helm belt out "The Night They Drove Ole Dixie Down," I became a fan for life.

After the concert, we made our way to the party at Greg Shanklin's. When we arrived, we found out somebody had showed up with a bottle of Quaaludes. They were the drug of choice for the crowd I ran with and pretty popular among all of the town's tow truck drivers. When Quaaludes came to Hattiesburg, you could guarantee two things: one, they would sell out fast, and two, there would be a lot of wrecked cars the next morning. We each bought a couple, and the night was on. We both took one and started drinking heavily while watching a movie where people were fighting with nothing on their hands but washcloths.

After we downed a few beers, the Quaaludes were kicking in and the washcloth fighting started looking like fun. We got a couple of washcloths from the bathroom, found an empty bedroom, and went at it. We were nailing each other in the face, and I was holding my own. This was a bit surprising because Charles was older and much tougher than me. Charles may have been pulling his punches or the painkiller I had taken was helping me absorb them, but we pounded away on each other for about ten minutes. Finally, he landed one square on my nose and dropped me like a rock. Blood started pouring from my nose, and it swelled up and turned purple. When I came to my senses, I was sitting on the couch in the living room and one of the prettiest girls in town, who was several years older than me, was taking care of me. If this is what would happen when I got my face smashed, I would gladly take all the beatings anybody wanted to give me. My nose eventually stopped bleeding and she quit playing nurse, so I went back to drinking as Charles took me around the house to show everybody his handiwork.

A little while later, the front door opened up and in walked Randy, my former best friend turned archnemesis. I decided to try to make amends and walked over and apologized for trying to give him the business at Lillie Burney. He accepted my apology, and we spent the next hour drinking and reminiscing. We decided to take a cruise and smoke some pot. We got in his car and headed for Highway 98, going west out of Hattiesburg. Highway 98 is four lanes now, but in the 1970s it was a two-lane road that mostly went through dark wooded areas. It had the well-earned name of Bloody 98 because of all the people who had died in car crashes. There were numerous cruises with planned routes through the country roads we would take to smoke pot. This one went west on Highway 98 to Bellevue, then left on Highway 589 until we got to Richburg Road, which we would take back into town.

We pulled onto 98 towards Bellevue. About seven miles out of town on a dark stretch of road, we saw flashing blue and red lights. As we got closer, we could see the road was full of highway patrol and Lamar County sheriff's cars. Then we came to a stop. It was apparent there had been an accident. One vehicle was in the right lane with the front smashed in. The other vehicle was sitting on the shoulder like it had been parked there. It was a yellow Ford Pinto with a black stripe on the side. I got out and ran toward the car. For some reason, the highway patrolman didn't say anything to me as I sprinted past him. As I reached the car, I could see the left front had been smashed into what looked like a perfect *V* shape. I got to the driver's side and looked in. It was Robert Spade and his girlfriend, Polly. At first, I didn't understand why they were sitting there. They looked like they weren't hurt, and the interior of the car was intact. He was just sitting in his seat like normal, and she was sitting in hers slightly leaning against the door with her arms in her lap. I leaned in and called his name. That's when I noticed a small trickle of blood streaming down his forehead and his eyes were wide open. I looked at her, and she didn't seem to have a scratch on her but her eyes were wide open too. I had never seen a dead person before, but I knew this is what it looked like. They were gone. They looked so peaceful sitting there, but they were gone.

Randy and I drove back to the party and gave everybody the news. The mood turned somber, and everybody started leaving to go home. Randy and I decided to keep riding around for a while. We drove around listening to Peter Frampton. This was the summer of *Frampton Comes Alive.* I don't know if there was ever an album that took off over a time period like that one. Every car you got into had it in the eight track. We drove around until the sun was about to come up then decided to call it a night.

Just as Randy turned onto Thirty-Fourth Avenue to take me home, we saw a car pulling up across from us. It was driven by Robby Spence, and sitting in the passenger seat was Bryant O'Connell. I immediately got the feeling that this would be a perfect time to settle whatever score we had to settle. He obviously did too, because as we pulled beside Robby's car, we both leaned forward and gave each other a "Let's do this" look. I shouted, "Behind Thames," and he shouted back, "Let's go." We pulled in by the monkey bars behind Thames school about fifty yards from where we first met. We both jumped out of the car and went straight for each other. This was not going to be a bro off. We were punching, kicking, and wrestling each other like a couple of wild animals. There were some hard feelings here, and we were determined to sort them out. This went on for about ten minutes until we ended up with each other in a headlock that we weren't letting go of.

There comes a time in any physical endeavor when you know you've had enough. We both reached it at the same time. I don't remember who spoke first, but one of us said, "I'll stop if you will," which was met with a quick "okay." Then we both collapsed on the ground. It took us a couple of minutes to catch our breath, but when we did, we just looked at each other and burst out laughing.

I said, "You know what's funny? We met just like this right over there," and pointed to the practice field where we first lined up against each other in practice. We started laughing again and gave each other a big hug. Bryant then said his parents were out of town and suggested we have a party that night. I agreed and told him I would call him that afternoon. The sun had now come up, and it was time to go home. I had been in two fights, had a broken nose, renewed two important friendships, and two families were getting a knock on the door that would change their lives forever. It was indeed time to go home.

We had the party at Bryant's house that night, and he told me he had just found out his family was moving to Florida before school started. We had a great time recounting everything we had been through but that was it for fire and dynamite. I would not see him again although we have connected on Facebook in the last couple of years. He has a great family and is the owner of a successful business in Florida. It also appears that he has developed a great faith in God. It's funny but that seems to be the case with most of the biggest heathens whom I knew.

CHAPTER 11

THE KING IS COMING

A week later, the moment I had been waiting years for arrived. My fifteenth birthday! What made this seminal event so special is that I was getting my driver's license. I was free at last. No more bumming rides, no more being dependent on others, and no more walking to the Minit Mart and sitting on my newspaper rack throne. I was now free to go where I wanted, when I wanted, and with whom I wanted, which basically meant I could pursue all the girls I wanted without having to deal with another guy just because he had a car.

My first car was a candy apple red Ford Mustang II. The Mustang II was another one of the American auto industries epic mistakes in line with the Chevy Vega. Like the Vega, you don't see any of them on the road today, but it suited my purpose just fine. It was a cool-looking car at the time and had a hatchback with fold down back seats in case I had the spontaneous need to recline. It also had a big purple sticker on the bumper that said, "The King Is Coming." I thought it was referring to Elvis. I didn't notice the cross and the ray of sunshine coming from the clouds in the background. Now the biggest heathen in Hattiesburg was cruising down the road with a bumper sticker promoting the second coming of Jesus Christ.

I drove that car through neighbor's yards, parked in flower beds, and went the wrong way down the busiest street in town. One night, around two o'clock in the morning, I attempted to make a right turn onto Hardy Street (Hattiesburg's main thoroughfare), but actually ended up going over to the lane that was heading in the opposite direction. I made it about a mile before stopping for some inexplicable reason. I just stopped in the middle of the road, put it in park, and fell asleep in the driver's seat. Fortunately, the first car to pass by had two of my friends in it, Pope Huff and Keith Overstreet. Keith was Van's older brother. They stopped and pulled me out of the car and put me in Keith's. Pope jumped in mine and turned it around and drove it to my house where Keith dropped me off. It was only by the grace of God that I didn't hurt somebody that night. I would need a lot of that over the next few years.

I didn't just keep it to driving dangerously either. One night, after homecoming, I decided I was going to use it to make a statement. I don't know what statement I intended to make, but like most of my other decisions, it just seemed like a good idea at the time. I dropped my date off at around one o'clock in the morning. I had been drinking heavily at the TEKE party we held after the homecoming game. On the way home, I got the bright idea to drive to the other side of town to Rowan High School and cut doughnuts on the football field. Rowan was the school that everyone in the tenth grade attended before moving on to Hattiesburg High for the final two years of high school. The football field was no longer in use, but it had a storied history.

Before integration, Rowan was the high school that almost all black students attended. Some of the greatest football players in NFL history had made their mark on that field. Now I was about to make mine. I pulled into the parking lot and stopped about twenty yards from the field. I revved the engine and took off. I slammed into an embankment as I got on the field and started spinning in circles from one end of the field to the other. It wasn't until the next morning that I realized I had lost the spoiler on my car in all the excitement.

The next Monday, as the bell finished ringing to start first period, I heard the familiar crack of the loudspeaker. "Would Pat McCool please come to the office?"

I walked into the principal's (Mr. Heath) office and took a seat across from his desk. This was one of those good news/bad news moments. The good news was that I wasn't going to have to buy a new spoiler because it was lying on Mr. Heath's desk. The bad news was that my spoiler was lying on Mr. Heath's desk and he had found it at the edge of the field where I had done all of my landscaping. Surprisingly, I didn't get in any trouble. Mr. Heath just gave me my spoiler back and asked me to refrain from doing things like that in the future. I picked it up and carried it down the hallway to the parking lot past the amused looks from my classmates and teachers. I had it reattached to my car, but it wouldn't be on there for long.

As the school year was ending, a friend was having a party at his parent's house on Richburg Road. We spent the night drinking until about one o'clock in the morning. That's when Brent Garry asked me and Mack Holmes if we wanted to go for a drive through the country. We hopped in his car, which was an old Chevelle with a powerful engine. The floorboard in the back where I was sitting had a large rotted hole where I could see the road as we drove over it. He started flying down those country roads as we chugged Bacardi 151 straight out of the bottle. We drove around for about an hour until we had finished off the bottle. We then headed back to the party, lucky that we hadn't killed ourselves, or anybody else. The night wasn't over though. I still had time to tempt fate.

I decided I'd had enough excitement for one night and got in my car and started home. I was in no condition to drive, but that had never stopped me before. I turned onto Arlington Loop, which was the road leading to the street where I lived. As I got about one fourth of a mile from the street that led to my house, I decided I wanted some chicken. The chicken and potato logs at the 7-Eleven on Hardy Street were the perfect meal after downing half a bottle of 151 proof rum. So instead of taking a right turn towards home, I hung a left and floored it.

I'm not sure if the alcohol had removed whatever sense I had left or if I was just in a hurry to get some chicken, but I pressed the gas pedal to the floorboard and held it there. When I got to Southampton Road, I didn't have the slightest chance of making the turn. I went straight across it at about one hundred miles per hour and hit the embankment where a telephone pole guide wire was attached to the ground. The car flipped end over end and sailed about thirty yards into a vacant lot before landing upside down. As the car flew through the air, I had this helpless feeling. There was nothing I could do but wait for it to land and see what the impact was going to do to me. It did nothing to me. When the car finally landed in a heap of twisted metal and broken glass, I was lying inside the car staring up at the seats and steering wheel without a scratch on me. The roof of the car had been completely crushed, except for one place, the place where I was sitting.

I pulled myself out of the car and walked to the road. I noticed it was very dark. This was two o'clock in the morning, but it was a populated neighborhood and I couldn't see a light anywhere. All I could see was what looked like the entire cast of *Night of the Living Dead* walking toward me. It turns out the telephone pole to which the guide wire was attached held the transformer for the neighborhood. It blew when I hit the wire, so I had knocked the power out for the entire neighborhood. They were all now coming down the street in their pajamas and robes to see who was responsible for them spending the rest of the night without air conditioning.

One of the first people to arrive was the district attorney for Forrest County. He was a friend of my dad's and lived five houses away. This would actually turn out to be a good thing because a couple of minutes later, a less sympathetic group showed up, the Hattiesburg Police Department. The officer asked me what happened, and I told him, and what I told him made no sense at all. I told them I had been run off the road by ten men in a yellow Cadillac. He asked me how fast I was going, and I told him just a few miles over the thirty mile an hour limit.

The officer then walked over to talk to my dad, who had just arrived, and the district attorney. While they were talking, I realized the story I told was physically impossible. There was no way my car could have landed where it did coming from the direction I said and acting like I counted ten heads in that car while I was flying through the air was way too much information. The police officer knew it too and did what police do when they're questioning morons. He asked me to tell the story again. I completely changed the direction of my car and the street I was coming from.

As my friend Scott Ray's mother told me a week later, "Pat, honey, you had us going until you changed directions." The police officer walked back over to my dad and the district attorney, and they talked for a minute. My dad then motioned for me and said, "Come on let's go home." I was shocked that I wasn't going to the police station for a breathalyzer. The alcohol vapor coming out of my mouth would have caught fire if somebody had struck a match. For whatever reason, they just let me go home and sleep it off. I didn't even get a ticket.

The next day, a friend of mine took me to the junkyard where my car had been towed, to get my eight-track tapes. I couldn't believe it when I saw it. The front was smashed halfway to the dashboard, and the roof was completely collapsed except for the small opening where I pulled myself out. I couldn't even get in the car to get my tapes. As we were staring at the car, one of the junkyard workers walked up. He asked if we knew the person who was driving that car. I told him he was looking at him. He said there was no way I could have been in that car and still be in one piece. I assured him it was me who had been in the car. He shook his head and said I was lucky there was no one in the passenger seat because they certainly wouldn't have crawled out. It would be years before I realized there was somebody in that passenger seat, and if he hadn't been there, I wouldn't have crawled out either.

CHAPTER 12

WORDS MATTER!

A few weeks later, I got my next car. It was also a Mustang II, but this was a silver blue coupe with a white landau top. It wasn't as cool as the last one but the landau top gave it a little more class, and I definitely could have used a little more class. The principal at my school also thought I could have used a little more class. A month later, I started the tenth grade, again. The Hattiesburg School system wasn't feeling as benevolent as they were the year before and wanted me to actually pass my classes. This was especially difficult for me because I wasn't attending them. I had developed a habit of coming for the morning classes and then leaving or coming late and not staying long. Sometimes I just didn't come at all.

A couple of months into the year the new principal, Mr. Radcliff, called me to his office. I didn't know what I had done to warrant this visit but I was sure it was something. He was being overly friendly as he asked me to take a seat. I sat down, and he asked how I was doing. I told him I was fine and then came the unexpected.

He politely said, "Pat, I didn't call you in here to get on to you about anything. We just want you to come to class."

I thought to myself, Wait a minute. He's asking me to come to class?

While I really appreciated his concern for my educational needs, the fact that he was "asking" me let me know there would be no consequences if I didn't. I told him I would and took what he said under consideration, but I went right back to my old routine. It was like most of the teachers and principals in the school system had heard of my reputation and were in some way scared of me. Most of them, but not all of them.

There was one teacher who wasn't the least bit intimidated by me. She was a short woman in her early thirties with black hair and a Toni Tenile–style haircut. Her name was Mrs. Hudson, and she was my history teacher. When I did go to class, I went to hers. I don't know what drew me to her class, her or the fact that I had an affinity for history. I would actually read my history book while I was lounging around Lake Shelby when I should have been in school. History was my second period class, and my normal routine would be to skip first period and show up for second and then stick around for a class or two before leaving for the day. Sometimes I would leave right after her class or just not show up at all.

One day, I got to her class a few minutes after the bell had rung. I was smelling like I had just come from Woodstock. I slipped into her class and tried to quietly make my way to my seat in the back of the room next to my buddy Scott Graham. Just as I was taking my seat, she spoke to me. This was not what I wanted. Surely she is about to call me out for the aroma wafting from my clothes. I usually slipped in and out of my classes without having attention drawn to me and didn't understand why she hadn't gotten the memo.

"Good morning, Pat!" she said with a huge smile on her face. "I'm so glad you joined us today."

I didn't know what was going on and just grinned and said, "Glad to be here."

I thought I had ended the conversation. She wasn't finished. She said, "Pat, I don't know what it is about you but I like you!" Then again, "I don't know what it is but I really like you!" I was stunned and just stood there grinning. I didn't know what she was saying or why she was saying it, but I never forgot it.

I don't think there is a month that goes by that at some point I don't stop and remember what she said that day. As I look back on it now, I know that this wasn't some spontaneous comment. She walked into school each day waiting for the opportunity to say that to me, to tell me there was nothing scary about me at all, but I was just a crazy teenager doing stupid things. She took the time to try to make a difference in my life. It stuck with me and now that comment is making a difference in other people's lives.

CHAPTER 13

HEARTACHE AND HEADACHE

I didn't get in any trouble the rest of the year, and I only had one car wreck. I had a car full of girls and figured a great way to impress them would be to fly around a school bus at a high rate of speed. Everything would have gone according to plan if that farmer hadn't placed the fence that I slammed into where he did. Fortunately, no one was hurt. After a couple weeks in the body shop, my car was good to go. I was actually making an effort to stay out of trouble for the first time in years. There was a simple explanation for this. I had a girlfriend. I had known her for several years. Her sister and my brother, Mike, were good friends. Her father was one of the most well-known men in town. Even though Hattiesburg was a small southern town, he was a nationally known lawyer. It wasn't unusual for him to fly across the country to represent some well-heeled client.

When we met, she was one year behind me in school. She was in the seventh grade, and I was in the eighth. Thanks to my academic prowess, she had now caught up to me during my second swipe at the tenth, and Mother Nature had caught up with her. We started dating during the fall, and by midyear I was in full blown teenage love. It wasn't going to last, and this shouldn't have come as a big surprise. I was headed straight for the top of my future GED class, and she would eventually become an attorney.

I was crushed the following summer when she informed me she was going to New York to live with a close family friend and attend the eleventh grade. This turned to full-blown despair once she got there and I found out that the friend's cousin, an up-and-coming rock star, was living right down the hall from her. I went to sleep every night wondering what was going on in that house. She broke up with me a few weeks after she got there. She started dating some Italian guy. I learned this at the same time she broke up with me. I never understood why women did that. "Uh hi, I'm breaking up with you, and dating an Italian guy named Marco. They call him the Italian Stallion." Some information is better served in pieces. It didn't matter either way. I was seventeen and thought the world was coming to an end. At least I didn't have to worry about turning to drugs and alcohol.

Even though I had my heart ripped out and stomped on, the summer did bring some good news. The Hattiesburg School System had a policy that wouldn't allow a student to remain in one grade for more than two years. I felt like this was a well-thought-out rule, and it had my full support because it meant I was now on my way to the eleventh grade without passing a class.

I didn't wreck a car that year, but I did almost kill myself by falling off one that was traveling at a high rate of speed. I was riding around with my good friend Greg Carpenter in his late 1960s model Chevy Camaro. It was one of those cars that, if he had kept it, would be worth about $50,000 today. We pulled up beside another friend, Lanny, who had a similar Camaro. I got out of the car and started talking to Lanny and the other guys in the car with him. A few minutes later, Greg got tired of waiting and told me to get in the car or he was going to leave. I kept talking. A couple of minutes later, Greg gave me one more chance to get into the car. I didn't take it, so he drove off.

He stopped at the end of the street to give me a chance to catch up with him. Lanny told me to hop on his hood and he'd drive me to the end of the street where Greg was waiting. Seemed like a good idea at the time. What I wasn't counting on was how quickly Lanny intended to get me to Greg's car. I hopped onto the driver's side of the hood and held on to the opening in his sunroof. He floored it. To make matters worse, he had just waxed the car and I started to slide off. I screamed for him to stop. He didn't. He thought the panic attack I was having on his hood was actually funny and sped up.

When he reached about fifty miles an hour, I knew I was heading for the pavement. I had to quickly figure out the best way to dismount from the hood of his speeding car. I could either slide off, which I was sure would cause my feet to go under the wheels, or I could push as I fell to try to clear the car. I pushed. My feet hit the asphalt first, followed by my face, then the back of my head as I flipped down the road. I flipped back over onto my face one more time before I rolled to a bloody stop in the middle of the street. Lanny thought he had killed me and jumped out of his car in a panic. Greg saw what had happened and turned around and drove back.

I was hurt. I just didn't know how badly. I was waiting for the reaction of Greg, Lanny, and the other guys who were there to give me a clue as to what kind of condition I was in. Lanny was screaming hysterically, so I was hoping somebody would give me a second opinion. That somebody would be Michael Wayne Lee, AKA M-Dubya, who had been in the car with me and Greg. M-Dubya was known for great philosophical quotes like, "Cereal is the nearest thing to nothin' you can get and still call it food."

As I regained consciousness I said, "I think I need to get to the hospital," which wouldn't have taken long because we were on the road that ran beside the hospital.

M-Dubya noticed this and said, "Well heck, McCool, if you had rolled five more times you would have been at the emergency room." I wanted to punch him in the face. I was lying on the ground with blood pouring out of my head and he was trying to be funny. I later realized that he was just trying to keep me calm. M-Dubya figured that cracking jokes would be more helpful in keeping me from going into shock than Lanny running around planning my funeral.

They piled me into the front seat of Greg's car and drove around to the Minit Mart, which was around the corner on the other side of the hospital. A curious crowd gathered around the car as we pulled up, to find out why my head looked like a soccer ball. The first person to stick their head in the car was my former girlfriend, Kim. Her eyes got big, and she put her hand over her mouth to keep from throwing up. Now it was time to go into shock. When I saw her reaction, I started shaking uncontrollably. Greg decided it was time to visit the emergency room. The nurses immediately put me on a gurney and rushed me back to see the attending physician who was my friend's father. The visit to the hospital turned out to be a good choice since I had suffered a major concussion and needed stitches in three places on my head to stop the bleeding. I was going to live, but I would have to stay in the hospital for eight days.

I was happy I was going to come through this with nothing more than a few scars on my head, but I wasn't happy that I had to stay in the hospital for over a week. The main reason for my distress was because the following night Southern Miss was playing the Ole Miss Rebels in Jackson, Mississippi. They were our most hated rival. They were the school that was born first and had all the money and the Southeastern Conference patch on their uniforms. Watching the Golden Eagles lay a beating on them was one of life's great joys. It's hard for people from other parts of the country to understand how important college football is in the south. Bonds are formed for lifetimes, families are drawn together, and neighbors hate neighbors over it.

Becoming a fan of the University of Southern Mississippi Golden Eagles was one of the best things to ever happen to me. It was the first thing I had an interest in as a teenager, other than girls, that wasn't immoral or illegal. It was also the main thing that eventually patched up the relationship with my dad and me. From the age of twenty-one until I moved to the New York area, we sat beside each other at every home game and made numerous road trips together.

We had beaten the Rebels the year before, and I planned on being there to watch if we beat them again. I just had to figure out how to get the IV out of my arm and get out of that hospital in time for kick off. So I devised a plan. Greg would go by my house and pick up my four tickets from my dad. He would then go home and call me when he was ready to leave for the game. I would then pull the IV out of my arm when the nurses weren't around and head for the fourth floor fire escape. Greg would wait at the bottom of the fire escape as I scaled down it. I would then jump in his car and off we would go to Veterans Memorial Stadium to cheer the Golden Eagles on to victory. I knew this was a stupid plan, but most of my plans back then were stupid so I was undeterred. The main hitch was that Greg thought it was stupid too. So he went by and picked up my tickets and took off for the game without me.

I listened that night on the radio from my hospital bed. The nurse had to tell me to keep it down a couple of times when I got a little too excited. The game came down to the final seconds with the Golden Eagles perched inside the five-yard line about to score the winning touchdown. I was sitting up in bed, waiting for Bill Goodrich, Southern Miss's radio announcer, to call the game winning play. It didn't happen. Our quarterback threw an interception on the last play and the Ole Miss player who picked it off was running free for the end zone, but the excitement hadn't quite ended at that point. In what would go down as one of the truly notorious moments in Southern Miss history, one of the Golden Eagle players, James Hale, who was standing on the sidelines with tears in his eyes, ran onto the field and flattened the Ole Miss player as he ran toward the end zone. Pandemonium ensued as half the Ole Miss team sprinted across the field led by their head coach, Steve Sloan. I guess James just didn't like losing that badly, but they did lose and I spent the next seven days in the hospital.

My stay at Forrest General Hospital finally came to an end, and it wasn't a moment too soon. That night the Mississippi State Bulldogs were coming to town to play the Golden Eagles. Everything I said about the Ole Miss Rebels could be said about Mississippi State. The only thing as sweet as beating the Rebels was beating the Bulldogs, and I planned to be there to watch it happen even though the doctor told me to go home and rest. There would be no last second interceptions or players coming off the sidelines to start a ruckus tonight. The Golden Eagles would come from behind and win the game, and the celebration was on. The best way we had found to celebrate a great victory was to down a bottle of Old Charter ten-year-old bourbon, and we didn't wait for the game to end to get started.

Later that night, Greg and I ended up at a party in downtown Hattiesburg. Greg was ready to go home and got a ride from someone. I decided to stay until I had the lamp shade firmly planted on my head. The party finally ended, and it was time for me to go home.

Unlike Greg, I didn't need a ride home. I had my car and I would be attempting to drive it. I made it out of downtown okay, but the long stretch down Hardy Street to my neighborhood was going to be a challenge. From my vantage point, the normally four lane Hardy Street had become eight lanes and I was having a hard time figuring out which one I needed to be in. I decided the best way to keep my car going in a straight line was to straddle the two yellow stripes in the center of the road.

This worked for a mile or two, but using all my energy focusing on the two yellow stripes prevented me from noticing all the red lights I was running. Unfortunately for me, the Hattiesburg police weren't having to focus on those yellow stripes and they noticed every one of them. They pulled me over, handcuffed me, and put me in the police car without bothering to give me a chance to walk a straight line. When I got to the police station, I decided I wasn't going to blow into the breathalyzer machine. I'm sure one of my legal expert buddies had convinced me this was the best way to handle the situation. It wasn't. A sheriff's deputy pulled a blackjack, which is a slender leather strap with metal in it, from his pocket and then smacked me across the face with it. I almost passed out from the pain that shot through my head. This was not what somebody that had just gotten out of the hospital from a major concussion needed. So I reconsidered my decision not to take the breathalyzer and blew a 2.30, which was about double the legal limit for DWI.

The next morning, I woke up in the jail cell with a massive headache. I didn't know if it was from the concussion, the smack to my head, or the bottle of Old Charter I had polished off the night before. It didn't matter. I had other problems. The DWI that I was facing was definitely a big problem, but it wasn't my biggest. My biggest problem was there were bags of marijuana in the trunk of my car when they arrested me. I didn't know if the police had found them, and I had no way to find out. I couldn't call the guard over to my cell and ask him if I was arrested just for the DWI or if they found the eight bags of marijuana in my trunk.

One thing I had going for me was I had lost the key to my trunk and the ignition key wouldn't open it. That was the main reason I kept the pot there in the first place. My friends and I would tie a string to the contraband and throw it to the back of the trunk. This meant if somebody was going to find it, they would have to know to pull the string or pry the trunk open. My jail cell window looked out over the parking lot. I looked through the small window and saw my car. There were no signs my trunk had been pried open. So I had to wait until my dad came to get me to find out how much trouble I was in. He got me out later that afternoon, and on the ride home I started my query.

"So, what are they charging me with?"

He looked at me in disbelief and said, "Well, they sure as heck aren't just giving you a ticket for running a red light." I knew then that I was just getting charged with a DWI and running four red lights.

Once again, luck was on my side. The judge was my next-door neighbor and good friends with my dad. I got my license suspended for six weeks until I completed the Mississippi Alcohol Safety Awareness Program, also known as MASAP. This was not a class that I was inclined to skip. I also soon found out that I would be able to share a ride to class with my good friend Brody, who also tried to weave home that night. I learned a lot in those six weeks. I learned about the dangers of driving intoxicated and how alcohol absorbs in the bloodstream. I also learned that several of my friends' parents drove drunk too, because they were sitting in the back of the classroom trying to hide their faces the whole six weeks. Brody and I never told anybody, though. We figured it was an honor among thieves thing. What happened in MASAP, stayed in MASAP.

CHAPTER 14

YEP . . . THAT WAS SOME WAR

As the year progressed my old habits returned. I was not going to class. I had started the eleventh grade with great intentions. I was convinced that this would be the year I made my academic move. I went every day for the first few weeks, then started going sporadically, then not at all. I don't know what it was, but school was like a prison to me. I just couldn't make myself go. I finally decided it was time to end this charade altogether and officially quit. Now I could use all of my free time planning for my future, and that's what I did.

Most of my friends were making plans for life after high school themselves. Many of them were planning on going to college. Since I was not one to set my sights low, I decided that would be a great plan for me too. Not letting the fact that I had not paid attention in school whatsoever for the last four years deter me, I put my plan in motion. Since I had formally withdrawn from school, which was legal in Mississippi if you were over sixteen, I could take my GED, which I did, and aced it. I then took my ACT and aced it too. I made a 23, which wasn't going to get me into Princeton, but it was 5 points over what I needed to be admitted to a public university. The guidance counselor at Hattiesburg High School was shocked when she got my test result. She called to tell me how proud she was and that she always knew I could do it if I applied myself. I don't think I ever met the woman and had no idea who she was, but I appreciated the encouragement.

Four months later, I enrolled at the University of Southern Mississippi right along with all my former classmates that had spent the last four years actually going to class and paying attention. I signed up for twelve hours, which was four classes. American History 101, Political Science 101, Pre-Law, and something called Math 099. It seems I was so deficient in math skills that I had to take a class that I wouldn't get credit for just to gain enough knowledge to take an actual college math course. Two weeks into the year, my lack of preparation came back to haunt me. My American History 101 professor told the class we would be having our first exam on Friday and to make sure we went by the bookstore and got our blue books. I had no idea what a blue book was.

I went to the bookstore and told the girl behind the counter that I needed a blue book. She handed me a small blue book with blank pages. I still had no idea what this was for, but it had the words *blue book* on the front, so I felt like I was good to go. On the day of the exam, the professor walked in and wrote on the board, "In one thousand words, explain the French and Indian War." Whoa, you mean I actually have to know this stuff? No multiple guesses or boxes to check? I was obviously supposed to write down everything I knew about the French and Indian War, which unfortunately for me was nothing. I had spent the first two weeks of college focusing on what I thought was its most positive aspect. I was surrounded by two thousand eighteen-year-old females who were away from home for the first time in their lives.

I looked around the room and saw everyone writing diligently on the blank pages of their blue books. Not wanting to look like an idiot, I began to do the same. I knew nothing about this subject but that wasn't going to stop me from trying to appear as if I did. I started off with "The French and Indian War was a very interesting war. One of the most interesting aspects of the war was that it involved the French and the Indians." That was 28 words and I only had 972 to go. The professor was either going to think I was a total genius or a complete fool. He picked the latter. I got an F on the test along with a note suggesting I take a remedial English class. Not liking the chemistry that was developing with this guy, I dropped the class, but

I did pass my other two. I didn't study much in the classes I passed but did do the one thing that I had struggled with my entire scholastic career. I showed up. It's funny how that works out in college and life in general. People give you a lot of credit for just showing up.

I almost didn't get credit for showing up in one of the classes. My Political Science 101 professor was one of the most popular professors on campus. There was one thing that set him apart from all the other professors—he was blind. A couple of weeks into the year, the guy who sat beside me pointed out that if we left after the roll was called, he wouldn't notice. That made sense to me. So about seven of us who sat in the back of the class started showing up for roll, answering when our name was called, and then quietly slipping out of the back door. Sure enough, he didn't notice, but his assistant did.

We should have known that if a desk had a live human being sitting in it one minute and then nobody sitting in it the next, someone might notice. At the beginning of class on the day of our final exam, he said he had an announcement to make. He said that throughout the semester, some of us had taken the liberty to leave after roll was called and he assumed that meant we didn't want to be there so he just went ahead and marked us absent. Oh no! If he did that I was toast. You could only miss so many days before you failed and I had left every day since the third week of class. Fortunately for me and the other Houdinis who pulled the disappearing act, he was just messing with us.

Things were going well in the fall of 1979. I only earned a couple of credits, but I was going to school and actually passing classes. I had my own bachelor pad with a bright yellow Naugahyde couch and a parachute nailed to the ceiling in the bedroom. I didn't have to go very far to find a party because there was always one happening at my place.

I also got a new car that year. Well, I actually got two new cars because I totaled the first one. At the beginning of the summer, my Mustang II had finally worn out, so I got a white Volkswagen Scirocco Sidewinder with a big black stripe on the hood and rattlesnake decals on the side. This was a really cool car, but it was no match for the parked one that I slammed it into. We had a keg party at my house the night before and still had some beer left in the keg. Dave Evans and I thought it would be a great idea to put the keg in the back of my car and go cruising through town. We also thought it would be a great idea to take a Quaalude before we left. Neither one of those was a great idea. We made it halfway through our neighborhood when we turned onto Prince George Road where a friend was having a party at his house.

We weren't planning on stopping at the party and wouldn't have if one of the attendees hadn't recklessly parked her car on the street in front of his house. I remember turning onto the street and hearing Pink Floyd blaring from the two Bose speakers sitting in my backseat. The next thing I knew, I heard a loud crashing noise and felt the car come to an abrupt halt. The Pontiac Grand Prix that had been recklessly parked in front of the house barely had a scratch on it, but my VW was a smoldering heap. Dave and I weren't hurt either except for a bleeding gash on Dave's forehead when his head smashed my windshield. He actually apologized for breaking my windshield. What a guy! His first reaction to me almost killing him was to say he was sorry for damaging my car with his head.

Since we didn't worry about little things like learning from our mistakes, one month later, we gave driving unconscious another shot. This time, it was Dave's turn. The Golden Eagles were playing Ole Miss in Jackson. I borrowed my mother's Mercury Marquis because my car was in the junkyard. We checked off our list of game day supplies. One bottle of Old Charter ten-year-old, two joints (one for each leg of the journey), and Warren Zevon's latest cassette, which we planned on listening to on the victorious ride home. We also decided to bring along a couple of Quaaludes just in case we lost the game and needed something to ease our pain. The last decision would prove costly.

Dad, as usual, had given me the tickets and the seats were on the aisle one row behind him and his friends. As we sat down, the bottle of Old Charter slipped out of the jacket I had worn to smuggle it into the stadium and started rolling down the steps. I ran down and caught it before it smashed into the concrete at the bottom. I was relieved to have saved our refreshments but now I had to stroll back up the stairs holding a bottle of bourbon for everybody to see.

I walked past Dad and his friends. He shook his head but didn't say anything. I was eighteen and that was the legal drinking age in Mississippi at the time. You couldn't buy liquor at eighteen but you could drink it. Drinking bourbon at a college football game in the south was a time-honored tradition, so all was good and we got ready for kickoff.

The game went according to plan. The turning point was the opening kickoff and the Golden Eagles crushed the Rebels 38-8. I had done more celebrating during the game than Dave. I was also fresh off a head-on collision with a parked car, so we decided he should drive. The game had gone better than we had hoped, so there was no need to take any pills to ease our pain. Unfortunately, need was never the reason we took pills, so we took them anyway.

The next thing I remember I was at a party and upset because somebody wouldn't give me the keys to my car. I said in a loud and angry voice, "Just give me my keys and I'll go home."

I heard a deep voice reply, "Son, if you don't get out of that car before the highway patrol gets here, you won't be going home."

I had been dreaming when I asked for my keys. I wasn't dreaming when the deep voice told me to get out of the car. Not only was I not dreaming, but for some reason my head was under the steering wheel and I was staring at the gas and brake pedal. I pulled myself up, and the man with the deep voice helped me out of the car.

A guy, an acquaintance from school, was at the scene and gave us a ride home before the police showed up. He later explained what happened. He said as he was driving south on Highway 49 toward Hattiesburg, he approached a line of cars driving slowly in the right lane. He pulled into the left lane to pass the slow moving cars. As he got to the front of the line, he saw our car swerving from shoulder to shoulder, making it impossible to pass. He said this went on for about fifteen miles until we finally went down in the median and started clipping trees until we finally hit one large enough to stop the car. Apparently, Dave had fallen asleep and left the car on autopilot. We both got out of the car uninjured. We were very lucky that night, and it wasn't because we didn't get hurt. We were lucky because we didn't hurt anybody else.

Fate smiled on me and Dave that night as it did many other times during the years we ran together. There was a day coming though where fate wouldn't smile on him, and I will never forget it. I was driving down Lincoln Road, and Dave was in the passenger seat. I can remember exactly where we were when he turned to me with a puzzled look and said, "They haven't heard from Debbie." Debbie was Dave's older sister. She was my brother Mike's age, and they were good friends. I was also good friends with Dave's other sister Tami, so Mike and I both knew their family well. Debbie was a student at Southern Miss and lived with another girl in a house outside of town.

I asked him what he meant, and he said they (his parents) had not heard from Debbie in a couple of days. He said one possibility was that she may have gone to New Orleans with her boyfriend, but it was unusual for her not to tell somebody. I thought it was odd myself but figured there was a good explanation for it and told Dave that she would probably turn up soon.

"I hope so," he said.

We then changed the subject and went on with the night's events. I dropped him off at his house around one o'clock in the morning and went home and went to sleep. My mother woke me up at six o'clock the next morning to tell me that Dave was on the phone. I had no idea why he would be calling me at six o'clock, but I got up and headed for the kitchen and grabbed the phone.

He said, "They found Debbie. She's been murdered."

I drove over to Dave's house as the sun was coming up, but there was nothing I could say or do. There was nothing anybody could say or do to end the nightmare to which his family had awoken. A well-meaning crowd had started to gather at their house, but it soon became apparent that this wasn't helping. There really is nothing to say at a time like this. You just let people know that you love and care for them as best you can, and that's what the rest of Dave's friends and I did. There was a lot of speculation in the coming days as to what had happened. It ended up being two transient men who were passing through town and decided to rob a house. She just walked in on the wrong people at the wrong time. There are times when life doesn't make any sense, and this was one of those times.

96

CHAPTER 15

I'M GONNA BE ALL I CAN BE

In the spring of my freshman year, I cut my academic progress in half. I again signed up for twelve hours (four classes) but nixed every class that started before twelve by the drop/add date. I was having a lot of fun and didn't want to put a crimp in it by having to wake up before noon. This left me with one science class that started at seven o'clock in the evening and was held two nights a week. I was happy when I found out I had passed the class because I don't think the professor liked me very much.

One night, he was going on about how ridiculous it was that the school spent so much money on football when science was way more important. I pointed out that if he could hold a science class and have thirty thousand people pay thirty-five bucks a ticket to attend, the university might warm to his way of thinking. I do have to give him credit because the only things I remember learning in college came from his class. One was that if you didn't take a bowel movement when the urge presented itself, you would end up constipated. The other was that most people who were reported to have died in their sleep actually had a heart attack while having relations. I don't know if that's true or not, but every time I hear of somebody passing that way, I get a little suspicious.

By the end of the spring semester, my march toward a degree in business administration was going at a snail's pace. At the rate I was going, I would be old enough to retire the day I received my diploma. I took a hard look at my situation and decided I might need to go in a different direction. So I joined the army. It was time for me to be all I could be. I would spend the summer in basic training, then join a reserve unit at Camp Shelby outside of Hattiesburg, and enroll in ROTC at Southern Miss. I would then spend four years getting my degree and be commissioned as a first lieutenant in the United States Army.

I went to Fort Sill, Oklahoma for my basic training. This was where my dad had gone to basic training and the place my brother Mike was born. I had also lived there for a year during my early childhood. I was going to Fort Sill because I had signed up as a 13 Bravo, which was the MOS for the artillery. My dad was an artillery-man, so I decided to follow in his footsteps. Volunteering to join the artillery would also save me a lot of suspense in the reception station when I got there. The majority of guys enlisting in the army at that time were going to be either 13 Bravo (artillerymen) or 11 Bravo (infantrymen). They just didn't know it when they signed up.

The first thing you did when you arrived at basic training was spend three days at the reception station. You would take an aptitude test to see what special skill set you were suited for. Most of these guys had been told by their recruiter they were going into some highly specialized field that they could use for future employment when they got out of the army. Reality set in when test results came back. That's when most of them found out that instead of spending four years learning about advanced electronics, they would be cocking a cannon or shooting a rifle. It had to be disappointing when they realized the only thing they were going to be able to tell their future boss was they could kill a guy with a rifle at three hundred meters from a lying position.

Two weeks after I got to Fort Sill, I was running through the battery area. You ran everywhere you went unless you were in your flip-flops on the way to the shower. My drill sergeant stopped me and said the battery commander wanted to see me. I had no idea what this could be about. Other than being a little out of shape when I got there, I couldn't think of anything I had done wrong. I walked into the Captains office and took my position in front of his desk. He said "Where are you from Private McCool?" I said "Hattiesburg

Mississippi sir." He asked me if there was a college in Hattiesburg. I told him the University of Southern Mississippi was located there. He said "Yeah, I graduated there under your father. He's a good man." As I stepped out of his office I heard him tell my drill sergeant to look after that boy. I was six hundred miles from home in the United States Army and I was still benefiting from being the son of Lt. Colonel James M. McCool.

I did learn one valuable life lesson in basis training: It was easy to become the victim of your own wishful thinking. I was serving as platoon guide which meant I had access to the drill sergeant's office. I would sneak a peek at the training schedule on his desk every time I went there to see what was coming up. One day I was looking at the schedule and noticed there was nothing listed for what was to be the last two weeks of basic training. I thought this might mean we were going home two weeks early. I passed this along to some of the guys in my platoon.

A week later a couple of the guys came running into the barracks and told me I was right, we were getting out two weeks early. They said some guys in 2nd platoon had heard the same thing from the guys in 3rd platoon. so it had to be right. I was excited. I was so desperate to go home that I had drawn a timeline on the band holding the camouflage on my helmet and crossed off each day as it passed. I gleefully marked through the last two weeks and wrote HOME in its place. The day that we had decided we were going home finally came, and we weren't going anywhere. I had told the guys in my platoon (4th), and they had told the guys in 3rd platoon. They told the guys in 2nd platoon, who told the guys in my platoon that had heard it from me first. So when I found out that everybody in the whole battery thought we were going home early, I knew it had to be true, except it wasn't. It was just a rumor started by an idiot. Me!

The two weeks passed, and I graduated basic training. I had finally done something worthwhile. I flew home from Fort Sill knowing I was a new man, dedicated, disciplined, and determined to do the right thing. There would be no more excessive drinking, drug taking, or irresponsible behavior, until that night. I hooked up with my friends and headed to happy hour at a bar on Hardy Street called

Hardy Street Station. We started knocking back shots to celebrate my return and right on cue somebody showed up with some Quaaludes. I didn't have to worry about driving drunk that night because I didn't make it out of the parking lot before I became violently ill. I was home and I had picked up right where I left off.

I used the money I brought home from the army to rent a house outside of town with my good friend Craig. We would have parties every night, and everybody would show up, friends from the neighborhood to members of the Southern Miss football team. I had become friends with a few of the best players on what was one of Southern Miss's best defensive teams in history. They were stars on the team that smashed Florida State 58-14, broke Bear Bryant's 62 game winning streak in Tuscaloosa, and were ranked as high as number 9 in the country. I was having a blast, too much of a blast to notice the tsunami of bad decisions that was about to swallow me up.

A few weeks before the end of the semester, a friend of mine returned from a trip to Miami. He brought with him a large bag of cocaine. I hadn't snorted much cocaine and what I had wasn't that potent, so I wasn't that impressed with it. This was different. What was also different was the new way he had discovered to use it. In addition to the potent bag of cocaine, he also had a bag of hypodermic needles. I had always told myself that I would never stick a needle in my arm. I'm sure everyone whomever stuck a needle in their arm told themselves the same thing at some point. I figured I had nothing to lose, so I might as well give it a try.

My friend mixed the cocaine in a spoon and drew the liquid out through a cotton ball. One guy held a belt around my arm while he stuck the needle in my vein. He pulled it back slightly until he saw blood form in the syringe then pushed the needle until it was empty. At first I felt flush all over like I was about to throw up. Then the nausea was replaced by what sounded like a snare drum playing in my head, which was followed by the happiest and most content feeling I had ever felt. I would spend the next three months desperately trying to get that feeling again.

Everything changed overnight. From that point forward, I would spend everything I had chasing something that couldn't be caught. That's the dirty secret with addictive drugs. You're always trying to feel like you did the first time you took them, but it's never going to happen.

A few weeks later, the guy who brought the coke from Miami came over with another friend from the neighborhood, Rob. It was late at night, and we went into the back room. He was preparing the syringe, and I noticed he was putting an abnormally large amount of cocaine in the spoon. I asked him if he meant to do it, and he said he had gotten used to it so he needed a larger shot.

He took the shot and immediately began convulsing. His eyes glazed over, and he started flailing wildly like he was having a seizure. Rob and I panicked. We knew the right thing to do was call an ambulance. We also knew that doing the right thing would probably get us in a lot of trouble. All three of our fathers were well-known in town and there was a pretty good chance the ER doctor would know them. We made the cowardly choice and put our own interest above the life of our friend. We held him down on the floor to prevent him from flailing around and injuring himself. We just sat there holding him down and waited to see if he was going to live through this. He did. He not only survived that night, but survived cocaine and drugs altogether. He is now a medical doctor with a successful practice. Rob died ten years ago of a drug overdose.

I sold everything I could find to support my habit. My stereo and speakers went first. I think I even sold a love seat and two chairs. I finally decided the best way to have a lot of cocaine was to sell cocaine. The problem was, I didn't know a lot of people who bought or sold cocaine. I asked the guy Craig and I got our pot from if he knew where I could get some. Turns out he did—himself. I got him to sell me two ounces on credit. I was going to sell one and keep one. I just had to find somebody to buy the one I was selling. A friend of mine suggested we take it up to Ole Miss where another friend of ours was going to school. He said he could sell all the cocaine we could bring him.

We drove up to Oxford the next day and went into our friend's dorm room. He took one of the ounces and said he would be back in a little while. A little while turned to hours as we waited for him to bring the money back. He finally showed up six hours later, but he didn't have the money. He said a guy had taken the bag and was going to split it up, sell it, and bring him back the money, but he never came back. He said he would try to find the guy the next day, so we stayed the night in his dorm room. The next day he couldn't find him, nor the next. After two days, reality set in. He wasn't going to find the guy, and I wasn't getting the money. I now owed $3,000 to people who did not play around.

We returned home and I went to the house of the guy to whom I owed the money. I explained what happened and gave him eight hundred dollars, which was all the money I had. He didn't care what happened. He said I had until Friday to give him the rest and it would be settled by blood or money. I went back to my house to figure out what to do. I spent the whole night sitting on my couch with a blanket wrapped around me to keep warm. I had no heat because I had spent the gas bill money on drugs. The next morning, I woke up and made the worst decision of my life. I was going to try to rob a convenience store.

The way I decided to do this made no more sense than my decision to do it. I was going to bluff them into giving me the money in the cash register. I rolled up a sock and stuffed it in my pocket. I had recently seen the Unknown Comic on TV do his set with a paper bag over his head to conceal his identity and thought that could work for me too. I walked into the store, pointed at the bulge in my pocket, and told the clerk I had a hand grenade and to give me the money in the register. The clerk was a woman, a very scared woman. Her eyes got big. She clutched her chest, and said she had a heart problem in a trembling voice. I wasn't counting on this.

I decided to end this and turned toward the door to run out. That's when I got my second surprise. The male store owner had been kneeling down behind the counter when I walked in. He wasn't kneeling anymore and he had a gun, a large caliber gun. I ran out of the store across the parking lot toward the woods. I was hoping he wouldn't follow me and try to shoot me. My hopes were dashed when I heard the first gunshot. I was then hoping he was just shooting in the air to scare me. Those hopes were dashed too when I saw the pine tree explode in front of me as the second shot went off. I jumped over a fence leading to the woods and started down the hill as I heard a third shot. The scene from the movie *In Laws* where Peter Falk told Alan Arkin to serpentine while they were being shot at popped into my head, so I actually started zig zagging to the car I had parked on the highway. I jumped in and took off as I heard bullets bounce off the trunk of the car. When I got back to my house, the sheriff was waiting for me. They didn't know for sure it was me, but somebody saw me speeding down the highway so I was their top suspect. I confessed on the spot.

They booked me and put me in a cell. I had been in a jail cell before, but it was only for hours or days. This time it could be for years. This was the culmination of every bad decision I had ever made, but the beginning of every good decision I would make for the rest of my life.

An older inmate walked up to my cell. He was a trustee so he was free to walk around the jail. He seemed sympathetic and asked what I was in for and I told him. We talked for a few minutes before he reached into his pocket and pulled out a small red book. He handed it to me between the bars and suggested I read it. I asked him what was in it, and he said, "The answer to all your problems."

I sat on the cot and looked at the cover. It was a pocket-sized version of the Bible. I didn't read it that day. I was in too much despair to read anything. I just clutched it in my hands, looked up at the ceiling, and said, "God, if you are real, I'm ready to find out." No light came shining through the bars and no silhouette of Jesus appeared, but I felt something in that jail cell. It was the same feeling I had always gotten when I was in a bad situation. Just a feeling that something was always looking out for me.

The next morning, the guard came and opened the door of the cell. He told me to come with him. I assumed I was going for some routine appearance. I walked across to the sheriff's office, and the guard opened the door. Standing in the office were the two people who had always shown up when I was in a bind, my dad and my brother Mike. They were taking me home. Somehow Dad was able to post my bail. I would be a free man while I awaited trial, but that freedom wasn't likely to last. On the way to the car, I overheard the attorney who was talking with my dad say, "Oh he's definitely looking at some time. He could get up to fifteen years."

I spent that night with Mike. He was taking me to work with him the next morning. His father-in-law owned the largest manufacturing plant in Hattiesburg. So the next day, I went to work for his wife's family. They were great people. They always treated me like family regardless of what I had done, and I have never forgotten it. My supervisor was a petite woman who lived out in the country. She had a daughter named Karen who worked at the plant as well. My job was to do whatever Karen told me to do. By the second week of work, something was brewing between me and Karen. She was asking me to stay late for no particular reason. I didn't mind. She was attractive, and I certainly didn't have anywhere else to be.

A few weeks after my arrest, I was watching TV and saw an ad for a book written by former Dallas Cowboys coach Tom Landry. It was a book about God titled *The Book*. I don't know if he had given it that title because he didn't put any time into coming up with a name or because it just didn't need a name, but something compelled me to buy it. I had tried to read the Bible before but never got out of the "Begattitudes." All that begatting would wear me out and I would put it down. This book I couldn't put down, and I read it from start to finish. It explained things in a way that I could understand, and when I finished I decided from that point forward that I would believe in God. There is a big difference in knowing God is real and deciding to believe in him, but it would take me a while to figure that out.

Karen grew up going to a Pentecostal church, so believing in God was nothing new to her. As I was growing up, we went to church on occasion, but it wasn't a way of life. Karen told me one day that there was a spiritual person in every family and in mine it might just be me. I thought that was funny. If God wanted someone to carry his torch in my family, I was the least likely candidate.

The relationship between me and Karen became somewhat serious at one point. I grew close to her two young children: Erin, seven, and Tyler, five. Erin was just like her mother, and Tyler was a mischievous kid who reminded me of myself. We even talked about getting married. It wasn't to be though. She eventually dumped me for a guy with three kids of his own who worked in the oilfield. I think if I had been given the choice of marrying a guy who might be on his way to prison or a guy with a full-time job with benefits, I would have made the same decision. I talked to her several years ago and asked about the kids. She said Erin was happily married with a great family. Tyler had died years earlier in a drug lab explosion.

The months passed, and my court date was drawing closer. I tried not to think about it, but it was hanging over me like a guillotine. It was football season, so that was a bit of a distraction. The Golden Eagles played their last game of the season at home in a driving rainstorm. When the game ended, I slipped over the rail onto the field to talk to one of my friends on the team. He was a senior, and this was his last game at Southern Miss. He told me there was going to be a party at the sports arena and I should stop by.

I stayed at the party until it ended. When I got to my car, I realized I was fairly intoxicated. I had been drinking during the game and continued at the party. For some reason, I felt I would be better off if I walked home. It was a few mile walk from that part of campus to my house and it was still raining, but I decided to do it anyway. About halfway home as I was approaching a house, I saw a guy standing at the end of the driveway. He greeted me as I walked past.

"How are you doing?" he asked. I told him I was doing alright and asked him how he was doing.

He said, "You look troubled. Do you want to talk?" Nothing seemed odd at this point. I was drunk, soaking wet, and facing a prison sentence. It probably wasn't that much of a stretch to say I looked troubled. What happened next, though, got my attention.

I told him I would talk for a minute, and he invited me in. We walked toward a back room past a group of people sitting in the living room. I introduced myself. He said, "I know who you are."

Now somebody in Hattiesburg knowing who I was wouldn't be unusual at that time, but this guy wasn't from Hattiesburg, nor were the people in the other room. He was a student at Southern Miss from another part of the state. He continued, saying, "We've been praying for you."

"Who is we?" I asked.

"Me and those people in there," he said, pointing to the room we had walked past.

He said they were a student Christian group that met once a week at that house. Somebody brought my name up a while back, and they had been praying for me every week since then. He asked if he could pray for me, and I agreed. He prayed for me a few minutes, and I thanked him and got up to leave. I walked past the group in the other room. They all said they were glad I had come and to come back again. I never went back, but I never forgot the fact that total strangers cared enough about me to pray for my salvation.

Judgment day finally came. I would find out if I was going to spend the next years of my life locked in a cage. I did have one thing going for me. Several influential people had given character references on my behalf along with the guy who owned the store. I had gone by to see him and apologized several months earlier. He accepted my apology and wished me luck. As I was leaving, I thanked him for just shooting his gun to scare me and not trying to hit me.

He paused with a serious look on his face. He said, "I don't know what you're talking about. I did try to hit you. It was like the bullets were going right through you."

I parked my car behind the courthouse. As I got out, I took a long look at it, wondering if I would be driving it home. I walked in the courtroom and took a seat in the back. A few minutes later, I saw my attorney and two other men walk out of the judge's chamber. He motioned for me to follow him into a room on the side of the courtroom.

He closed the door as I stepped in and said, "We got it."

"We got what?" I asked.

"Probation. You're the luckiest guy I've ever represented!" he replied. I collapsed into a chair and put my head in my hands. I wanted to cry. "Here's the deal," he continued. "You plead guilty to simple robbery and you get five years probation. If you complete that successfully, they will expunge it from your record. But, if you screw up, you're gonna spend up to fifteen years in the state penitentiary."

I couldn't believe it. I was a cat who had used up nine lives and been given a tenth. I went outside and just stared at the blue sky. I didn't know why I was walking out of that courthouse, but I knew there was a reason. I was released from probation after three years for good behavior.

CHAPTER 16

I'LL SELL ANYTHING
BUT INSURANCE

I was now determined to make something of my life. I just had to figure out how to do it. I enrolled again at Southern Miss, but still had the same results. I signed up for three classes and only completed one. I probably hold the record at Southern Miss for enrolling the most times and making the least amount of progress. I had come to the realization that this wasn't going to get me anywhere. Besides, my academic adviser told me I was eventually going to have to pass a college math course and that just wasn't going to happen.

I started searching the want ads. I knew a GED and 12 college credits wouldn't make me the most desirable job candidate, but there was a path for me to success, and I was going to find it. While I was searching for that path, I went to work at an auto parts store driving around town in a truck with a huge yellow hat on the roof. It wasn't exactly the coolest job, but I wasn't worried about being cool anymore. One day I saw an ad in the paper for a sales job that paid up to five hundred dollars a week. I thought sales could be my ticket. If anybody could make a living with their mouth, it was me. I called and scheduled an appointment. I told myself if this job was anything but insurance, I wanted it. I knew I could sell anything but insurance.

It was insurance. It wasn't just any kind of insurance either. It was door-to-door and straight commission. Exactly what I said I would never do. So I took the job. Five hundred dollars a week was a lot of money back then, and something inside told me I could and should do it. It would be one of the best decisions I have ever made.

The owner of the company was an eccentric man with a tent revival hairdo. He lived in a house that looked like a castle with a limousine parked out front. I had passed that house many times on my way to my buddy M-Dubya's. It looked to me like he was one of the richest men in Mississippi, and I was now working for him. During my week of training, I met his youngest son who was going through training at the same time. We hit it off and became friends before the week was over. I also became friends with his older brother and sister, but the youngest son and I would become best friends over the next four years.

After I passed the insurance exam and completed training, I had a meeting with the owner. We talked for a minute and then he asked me if I believed in God. I told him I did. He then asked me if I had ever accepted Jesus as my Lord and Savior. I told him I hadn't. He asked me if I wanted to. I immediately thought to myself, "Hey, can somebody turn the AC on because it's getting warm in here?" Not only was I not expecting this, but I also had a bottle of Glenfiddich back at my apartment that I had no intention of letting go to waste. Without giving it any more thought, I said sure, so we hit a knee and started praying. When he was finished, there were no angels singing and I didn't start break-dancing around the office. I didn't notice it at the time but something was different. I continued with my same lifestyle, but some things that hadn't bothered me in the past would begin to bother me in the future.

On Monday, I went out with my sales manager, Carl, for my first day in the field. I had rehearsed my presentation and could recite it in my sleep—"Hi, I'm Pat McCool and I've been showing this to your neighbors and I believe it will interest you also. May I come in?"—and on it went. Carl was going to make the first presentation then I would do the next, if I was ready. We approached the first prospect, and he wasn't interested. That didn't stop Carl from going through the whole *War and Peace* version of the presentation. I didn't understand why you would waste time wearing somebody out who clearly wasn't interested but that was how it was supposed to be done.

I decided I would give the next one. I adjusted my new suit and made sure my clip-on tie was fastened in place. I knocked on the door, and the nice lady who answered invited us inside. We sat down at the kitchen table, and I opened my sales pad. A sharp pair of scissors fell out and stuck me on the arch of my foot. I didn't flinch from the pain, but I did break out in a sweat. I completely butchered the presentation, but she bought the policy anyway. I honestly think she felt sorry for me. I would never have a prospect feel sorry for me the rest of my insurance career, but it didn't matter. I had sold a policy and now knew I could do it.

The next day, I decided to go solo. I quickly ditched the canned sales pitch and developed my own. I also decided I would not waste time trying to put people in a head lock who clearly weren't interested in what I was selling. The nice lady the day before had proven to me that there were people who wanted what I was selling and I just had to find them. It worked. I sold another policy that day and one more before the week was over. By the next month, I had become one of the top salesmen in the company.

I started piling up "Salesman of the Month" trophies and filling my apartment with coffee makers, alarm clocks, and microwave ovens that I won at the monthly meetings. I spent four years with the company, and they were some of the best of my life to that point. I learned I could do anything I wanted if I applied myself. The most valuable lesson I learned was the best way to get attention was to make sacrifices and work hard. This was much better than the way I had done it in the past.

In my last year with the company, I won salesman of the month the first five months of the year. A new agent with sales experience had joined the company a few months back, and she was gunning for me. In the month of June, we had the biggest contest of the year and she was telling anybody who would listen she was going to win it. She had good reason to say it too because going into the last week of the month she was way ahead of me. It would take the best sales week I'd ever had for me to beat her.

On Monday morning, I woke and decided that if I was going down, I was going down swinging. I prayed for God to give me my best week ever and went to work. By that afternoon, I had sold three policies, which was the most I had ever sold in a day. The next day, I got up earlier and worked later. The next day, I worked even later. I was having the best week I had ever had but didn't tell anybody. Friday morning came and I was within striking distance, but I needed another three policy day to win. I knew what she had done that week because her sales manager was taunting me all week by telling me how much she sold each day. I knew three would do it because she was already declaring victory and taking the day off.

I sold two policies before noon on Friday. I just needed one more, but it would be elusive. I worked all that afternoon with no luck. It was getting late in the evening, and I was getting tired. Things were looking grim, and I started to consider giving up. I only considered it for a minute. I knew I wasn't trying to win an Olympic Gold medal, but this was important to me so I kept going. Two hours later, as the sun was going down, I sold that policy. I drove home with the theme from Rocky blaring in my head.

The next morning, the woman I was competing against walked in the room smiling and waving like she had just been crowned Miss America. She was already getting congratulations on the great month she'd had. I just sat and waited. When the time came to announce the winner, Tom, the guy who handled the contests, called us both to the front. Tom had a mischievous side and wanted to act like he was creating suspense, but he knew what was coming.

He set the trophy on the podium, and the woman immediately picked it up and launched into her victory speech. She was thanking everybody she could think of, God, Jesus, the owner of the company, and the woman who had provided food for the meeting. Tom finally had his fill of this and motioned for me to step forward. I think she had gotten around to thanking her ancestors by the time I snatched the trophy out of her hand. Even when Tom announced that I was in fact the winner, she still continued her speech. It wasn't until I began mine that reality finally set in that she hadn't won anything. I would like to say that I felt bad for her, but I would be lying.

After four years, I had a room full of trophies but I didn't have what I wanted the most, a bank account full of cash. What I got paid and what I thought I was going to get paid just never worked out. The comptroller of the company didn't care for me very much and would always find a way to take big deductions from my check. He resented my relationship with the owner's family and would cause me problems whenever he had the chance. The owner's oldest son told me if I got a chance to work somewhere else, I should take it. So I started looking for a better opportunity.

I might not have made the money I wanted, but my time working for the owner of that company was one of the best things to happen to me. It also gave me another chance to try my skills as a thespian. I attended the church he had helped build where he was the minister of music. When the Christmas play rolled around, he volunteered me to play one of the wise men. I knew I would be a perfect wise man. I didn't have to worry about cursing in the sanctuary like I had in the school auditorium because I didn't have a speaking part. All I had to do was walk on stage and hand my Frankincense to the baby Jesus and exit stage left, which I did flawlessly.

I also got to witness the International World Checker Championship. Yes, there is such a thing. The owner's house that looked like a castle was also the International Checker Hall of Fame. It had a large banquet room completely devoted to checkers with a checkerboard floor. People from all over the country would actually stop in to visit and buy souvenirs. Once a year, they held the World Championship of Checkers. Each year, a new challenger would show up to try and take down the defending champion, who was a sixty-something-year-old guy named Marion from Ohio who lived with his mother. As far as I know, Marion never gave up his crown.

The owner also left a lasting impression on me. Toward the end of my time there, we were talking in his office, I think at the time he knew I wouldn't be there much longer. He was sitting in his chair, looking up at the ceiling, and said "Pat, I don't know what it is, but God has something really big for you." He then looked out of the window with a puzzled look. "I'll be John Brown if I know what it is, but he's got something really big for you." Those words stuck with me like the words of my tenth grade history teacher. I believed what he said and was determined to find out what it was.

CHAPTER 17

PAT MCCOOL MEET CHRISTIE BRINKLEY

A few weeks later, I was getting ready to go to work. I began getting an odd feeling. I just didn't want to go to work that day. Not wanting to go to work was nothing unusual, but this was different. Something was telling me not to go. So I put on my running clothes and headed out on the street for a run. As I turned the first corner, I noticed a woman, who had worked for the same insurance company as I at one point, approaching a house. I said hello as I passed by, and she yelled for me to stop. I went back, and she said she had been wanting to talk to me. She told me she knew of a great opportunity for me with another insurance company if I ever decided to leave the one I was working for. What a coincidence! I had just decided to leave the company I was working for.

She told me to go to the Ramada Inn and talk to Gary or Stan. I felt a burning desire to do this, so I aborted my run, got dressed, and drove to the Ramada Inn. Stan wasn't there but Gary was. I introduced myself and told him why I was there. He offered me a job, and I took it on the spot. Two weeks later, I went to work for American Family Life Assurance of Columbus Georgia (Aflac). There would be no worrying about getting paid with Aflac. This was no door-to-door insurance company. This was the company that pioneered workplace marketing and at the time had a lead system for the type of policy I was selling. I started making over $1,000 a week, and my life started on a course that would take me places I never dreamed.

There was one more benefit from my time with my former company. During my last year with the company, I started seeing the best friend of the owner's youngest son's girlfriend. The relationship lasted a few months after I left the company, but eventually ended. A month after it ended for good, I got some life-changing news. She was going to give birth to my daughter, Marlee, which would be one of the greatest blessings of my life. I also had another kid about to enter my life, but this one was grown-up and would eventually become one of the most well-known people in America.

By the end of the year, things were going good. I was making more money than I had ever made, and the Golden Eagles had just finished one of their best seasons in years. They were on their way to a bowl game led by a kid from the coast with a funny name who could throw a football through a brick wall. One day, my friend Loren came by my house. Loren was a friend of mine and Dave's from the neighborhood. In high school, he drove an old Volkswagen station wagon with a bumper sticker on the back that said, "My other car is a Rolls Royce," which was actually true. His parents were two of the top surgeons in the state of Mississippi.

Loren asked me if I wanted to meet Brett Favre. To a Golden Eagle fan, this was like asking a kid if he wanted to meet Batman. He explained that Brett had found out his girlfriend was pregnant, which was pretty big news at the time. Loren knew I was acquainted with someone who had a close relationship with former NFL stars. He thought I might be able to give him some advice. He also got a big kick out of being able to introduce me to Southern Miss's biggest star. A few days later, he brought Brett by my house and we became friends.

I moved into a larger three-bedroom house a couple of weeks later, and Brett's brother Scott moved into one of the spare rooms. Scott was also a good football player. He was a much more highly recruited player than Brett coming out of high school. He signed a scholarship with Mississippi State, but it didn't work out. Brett would stay at my house sometimes when he wasn't with his girlfriend, Deanna, or staying in the football dorm during game week.

I met his parents and most of his immediate family. They lived at the end of Irvon Farve Road, which was supposed to be named after his dad, Irvin Favre, but the county misspelled his name on the sign. My house was on the road behind campus. The whole Favre family would come over on the morning of home games, and we would cook out in my backyard. This would eventually prove to be very beneficial in a way I wasn't expecting.

I traveled with them to a lot of memorable road games like Texas A&M, Florida State, and Louisville. The Louisville game was the one that ESPN replays when they have their *Greatest Plays* shows. On the last play of the game, Brett heaved the ball about sixty yards downfield and it bounced off one receiver's head and into the arms of another who ran it in for the game-winning touchdown. The summer before his junior year, he was getting a lot of national attention. It wasn't uncommon for the phone to ring at my house with a well-known sports writer on the other end wanting an interview with Brett.

About a month before the season started, a writer with *Sports Illustrated* wanted an interview and he wasn't calling. He was there. Back then Sports Illustrated was a big deal. We didn't have the Internet and fifty sports channels covering horse hockey from Australia or one thousand college kids blogging from their mom's basement. If you were a sports fan, you read *Sports Illustrated* and one of their top writers was in town. Not only was he in town but he was sitting in the backseat of the car, while Brett and I were cruising down Hardy Street. Later that night, he actually leaned over and said he could tell that I was a good influence on Brett. I didn't know what he was talking about. Influencing Brett was like trying to train an alligator. He was going to do what he was going to do.

There was one time I actually might have had an impact, but it was Brett's oldest daughter who would benefit. He called me at about one o'clock in the morning to tell me Deanna had gone into labor and he needed me to drive her to the hospital. I pointed out that she lived two blocks from the hospital and I would be glad to take her but didn't understand why that was necessary. He said the hospital was in Gulfport and the doctor said to bring her in right now. I asked him if he told the doctor she was seventy miles away in Hattiesburg. He didn't and I realized there was no point to this discussion and jumped in the car to go get her.

The reason I needed to drive was because the only car Brett had available was his dad's old Datsun truck. Datsuns were the forerunner to what today is a Nissan. This thing had four bald tires and one working headlight, not exactly the best vehicle to transport a woman in labor. I had a late model Toyota MR2 sports car, which wasn't exactly a maternity wagon itself. It only had two seats, and we could barely fit her in the car. To make matters worse, it was raining and foggy. He followed behind as we made the slow ride to Gulfport.

We finally made it to the hospital, and she delivered the baby about five hours later. While Brett and I were in the waiting room, I asked him what they were going to name her. He said they were thinking about Brettianna. I figured if there was ever a time I needed to try to change his mind, this was it.

I said, "I'm not so sure I would do that."

He said, "Why, you don't like it?"

"It's not that I don't like it, it's just that she might not like it."

I don't know if Deanna would have actually gone along with it in the first place, but they named her something else.

Southern Miss was set to open the season with third-ranked Florida State in Jacksonville. ABC was televising the game nationally. This was a big deal because back then every game wasn't on TV like they are today. Scott and I drove over the night before and stopped in Tallahassee. We had a big stack of "Favre 4 Heisman" bumper stickers, and we covered the Stop signs on Florida State's campus with them. I also found out the day before the game that my cousin Drew was going to make the traveling squad. Drew played center and was a walk on from Moss Point. He was a good football player and tough as nails, but he wasn't very big. Florida State was big. If he got in the game, he would be lining up against a future NFL defensive lineman.

FSU had pounded the Golden Eagles the year before. Deion Sanders picked off Brett's first pass of the game and took it in for a touchdown. It was all downhill after that. This game would be different. Deion had moved on to the NFL, and when the game began, it was clear the Eagles had come to play. There wasn't a guy on the Southern Miss sideline who didn't think they could win the game. Everybody on our side of the stadium thought we could win it too because we had number 4 directing the offense. The game went back and forth with each team taking the lead.

Late in the game, the Golden Eagles took the lead and our side was going wild. Then, with about seven minutes left in the game, FSU got the ball and started marching down the field. This was one of the best offenses in the country, and if we were to pull off the upset, our defense was going to have to stop them. They couldn't. With a little over two minutes left in the game, they scored the go-ahead touchdown. I was sitting on the first row behind the team bench with Scott and all his and Brett's buddies. We were devastated.

Then we saw Brett come running over in front of us and grab his helmet off the bench. He looked up at us with a huge smile on his face and shouted, "We're gonna win, watch this, we're gonna win!" Then he ran onto the field. They got the ball around their own twenty-yard line with over two minutes left in the game, and he went to work. They drove all the way inside the FSU five-yard line and had third and two with twenty-three seconds left in the game. He dropped back and almost got sacked, but avoided the pass rusher. Then he faded back a few steps and threw it to the tight end who was open in the end zone for the victory. I'm not so sure he didn't want Florida State to score, just so he could win the game that way.

One Friday, I was working in Columbia, Mississippi. It was the middle of the afternoon, and I needed directions to find my sales prospects. I went to the post office to see if the postmaster could help me out. I talked with him for a few minutes, and he gave me the help I needed. As I turned to walk out of the post office, I saw my former sales manager Carl leaning against the wall with a big smile on his face. I stopped and talked to him for about an hour. When we finished talking, it was around three o'clock, which was prime selling time for me. For some reason, I got the urge to call it a day. I had no intention of knocking off at three o'clock when I started the day, but something was pulling at me. That something would change my life forever.

I got home, sat down on the couch, and turned on the TV. Just as I was starting to feel guilty for taking the afternoon off, the phone rang. It was my district coordinator, Stan. Stan was a great help in getting me started with Aflac, and we had become friends. Stan is a country boy from Jones County and darn proud of it. He's also invented his own language. He's the author of many gems such as, "I had to tell him how the juice got in the coconut," and one of my favorites, "This is messedupper than a bent-wheel bicycle." Sometimes you had to think a minute about what he said, but when you did, it made perfect sense.

He told me I needed to come down to the office but wouldn't tell me why. At first, I refused but he persisted. I finally gave in and said, "All right, I'm coming down there, but when I get there, Christie Brinkley better be sitting on the couch!"

His voice raised a bit, and he said, "Okay, come on down." I drove down to the office, and he greeted me in the reception area. He had a big smile on his face as he opened the door to the next room and said, "Pat McCool, meet Christie Brinkley." I stepped into the room. Sitting on the couch was the most beautiful woman I had ever seen. It was the state coordinator's administrator, Gwen. I had heard about her from the other agents. They talked all the time about this beautiful woman in the state office. One guy even wrote her a two page poem, in calligraphy.

Everything they had said was true, but I didn't understand why he was introducing me to her because she was way out of my league. As I walked into the room trying to act as cool as possible, another agent walked in with her son who was coming to work for Aflac. We all looked at her as she introduced him.

She said, "This is Kenny, our new future number 1 salesman."

They walked into Gary's office, and I said "Yeah, and I'm gonna play center for the New York Knicks." I was the number 1 salesman, and there was no way this knucklehead was going to change that.

She said, "Ah, arrogance on the half shell."

I didn't know if she was insulting me or not, but the fact that she was talking to me gave me hope. I had to at least give it a shot, so I sat down and started making my move. A few minutes later, Stan walked back in and asked if we wanted to go get something to eat. I thought that was a great idea. We talked at the restaurant for a couple of hours and things were going well, but I didn't want to get my hopes too high. We all decided to go back to my house. A couple of hours later, the moment of truth came. Stan was getting ready to leave, and it was time to find out if she was buying what I was selling. If she left with him to have him drop her off at her hotel, it was over, but if she stayed to let me take her later, it was game on. She stayed.

I talked for the next six hours without shutting up. I stopped short of telling her that I had saved children from burning buildings and had a fortune stashed in the Cayman Islands, but I was laying it on thick and heavy. She laughed at everything I said. At one point, she put her hand over my mouth to get me to stop talking. It didn't work. I kept talking. I still am. The sun started to come up, and I finally had to take her to the hotel where she was staying because the Favre family would be showing up in a few hours.

Later that afternoon, the Golden Eagles put their annual beating on the Tulane Green Wave, but my mind was elsewhere. The next Monday, I went back to the office in hopes that Gwen would be there. She was, and we went back to the restaurant, this time alone. We talked for a couple of hours before she had to go back to Jackson where she lived. I asked her if she wanted to go to the Southern Miss game the next weekend. Luckily, she had to come back because she was in town for a sales promotion and they were finishing the following week. She said I could pick her up at her hotel that afternoon after they finished their meeting.

The following Saturday, Brett's family showed up at my house for the pregame cookout, and it's a good thing they did. Around noon, I got ready to pick up my date. It was game day, so I put on my lucky Southern Miss shirt. It was white with a big Golden Eagle logo on the chest and made out of 100 percent polyester. I was picking up the girl of my dreams and wanted her to know that I had class, so I put on my best dress shoes and dress pants to complete the outfit.

I walked through my living room where most of the Favre family was sitting on my way out. As I got to the door Brett's little sister, Brandy, who was sitting on the couch, said, "Wait a second, Pat, you can't do that."

"Can't do what?" I asked.

She said, "Never mind, I don't want to embarrass you."

I told her, "I would rather be embarrassed here than where I was going, so tell me what you're talking about." She said the shirt I was wearing didn't go with the pants and shoes I had on.

I asked her to follow me to my closet and pick out something that did. She picked out a dress shirt and said, "This will work." I asked her if she was sure, and she said she was positive. She was right.

Sometime later, Gwen and I were talking and she told me that one of the things she really liked about me was how well dressed I was the day I picked her up for that game. She said there was nothing more impressive than a man who knew how to dress. I took her back to my closet and showed her the shirt I intended to wear before Brandy staged an intervention. She said it probably would have been our last date. I don't know if that is true or not, but I am eternally grateful she was there to stop me from making a fool of myself.

It's a good thing Gwen was impressed with the way I was dressed because she couldn't have been impressed when she met part of my family later that day. After the game, we drove down to Mandeville, Louisiana to visit my brother Mike and his girlfriend. They had been drinking before we arrived, and when we went to a restaurant for dinner, they picked up where they had left off. Before the meal was over, Mike had kicked over a champagne bucket with an expensive bottle of champagne in it and eaten food off Gwen's plate, and his girlfriend had fallen down a steep flight of stairs. Mike eventually walked home alone and took the keys to the car with him so we had to get our waitress to drive us to his condo in her station wagon with his passed out girlfriend stuffed in the back.

My polyester shirt and ill-mannered brother obviously didn't scare Gwen off because we got married three months later. We got married in a double wide trailer in Smith County, Mississippi by a friend of mine with whom I had worked at my former company. His wife picked flowers from her garden, and his sons were witnesses. After the ceremony, he took us behind his trailer and showed us his mule and his goats. We then picked up a box of Popeye's Fried Chicken and headed home to begin our life together. We've been married twenty-eight years, and I thank God for her every day.

I also thank God every day for some other people who entered my life that day. Nicole and Devon, Gwen's daughters from a previous marriage. My daughter Marlee had been born a couple of months earlier, so I had a full family overnight. I was also swimming in a sea of estrogen. Girls are different from boys. I grew up with two abusive older brothers so I knew how to handle being around boys, but with girls I was clueless. I wasn't prepared for being around people who would burst into tears if you looked at them the wrong way. I actually think they raised me instead of me raising them. Either way, along with being married to my wife, the greatest joy of my life is knowing they love me and think I'm a pretty good guy.

Gwen polished me up in a hurry. She not only taught me how to dress, but set out on a lifelong mission to teach me to always do the right thing. She even made me stop lying. Lying is in a man's DNA. If a man is coming to your house and says he's thirty minutes away, you can guarantee he won't be there for an hour. If I told somebody I was going to do something, I would now actually have to do it. She taught me you have to treat people right and show them you care about them. She also brushed up my professionalism. I was one of the best salesman in the company, but my trunk looked like a recycling bin. It wasn't uncommon for Stan to call me asking about a client's policy. I would find it in my trunk covered in barbecue sauce. Gwen put a stop to that. I would sell the policies, and Gwen would handle the policyholders.

Now that my rough edges were smoothed out, I started climbing up the Aflac ladder. I was one of the top salesmen in the company for a year, then was promoted to District Sales Coordinator, then to Regional Sales Coordinator. Within two years we had taken one of the worst performing regions in the country and made it one of the top producing regions in the entire company. I was no longer winning ten-dollar coffee makers. I was now winning five-hundred-dollar briefcases and two-thousand dollar diamond rings. That was just the small stuff. We were also winning trips to Maui, Vancouver, Montreal, New York City, Honolulu, Caribbean cruises, and many other places we had never been. We were also making more money than we had ever made, and it was increasing every year.

As I reached my fifteenth year as a regional sales coordinator with Aflac, we lived in a nice house in one of the best neighborhoods in town with luxury cars in the garage. Most people would be satisfied with that, but I wasn't. I felt like something was pulling me but I would find out something was actually pushing me. I was in a meeting in Baton Rouge talking to some of my colleagues when the wife of my boss made what would turn out to be a fateful remark.

She said, "Listen to Pat, he just says things in such a funny way."

On the drive home, I couldn't stop thinking about what she said. Making people laugh had always come easy to me and I loved doing it. Numerous people throughout my life had jokingly remarked that I should be a comedian. It was definitely a joke though, because there was no way that was ever going to happen. I feared public speaking as much as anybody, and I would not ever do it intentionally. I had embarrassed myself enough for one lifetime, and there was no way I would risk doing it on purpose. When I found out that I was going to have to give a speech at an Aflac meeting, I would be sick to my stomach for weeks leading up to it.

The next month, I was driving to Baton Rouge for our monthly meeting. About twenty miles from town, a strange feeling came over me. I started feeling really hot and agitated. The feeling increased as I got closer to the meeting. Without really giving a lot of thought to it, I walked in my boss's office and quit. I don't think he believed I was serious. One of my fellow Regional Sales Coordinators later told me he held the position open for a month because he thought I was coming back. I didn't. I drove home that night and told Gwen that I had quit my job and was going to become a stand-up comedian.

I stared at her to see her response. If she told me that was the dumbest thing she had ever heard, I would go back the next day and beg for my job back. She didn't. She told me she knew I was going to quit the moment I pulled out of the driveway. She then told me that she prayed the whole time I was gone for God to give me direction and he had blessed me with the ability to make people laugh so I should use it. She was all in, so I was now going to become a comedian. I just had to figure out how to do it.

CHAPTER 18

PLEASE WELCOME . . .
PAT McCOOL!

I went online and Googled, "How do you become a comedian?" The answer was the same one I give people today who asked that question. Find the nearest comedy club with an open mic night, write five minutes of material, and go on stage and see if you're funny. That's exactly what I did. The nearest comedy club was the Stardome, which was three and a half hours away in Hoover, Alabama, a suburb of Birmingham. They held an open mic every two weeks on a Saturday night. I decided I would drive over to the next one and check it out. Gwen and I drove over the following Saturday. I met the woman who ran the show and scheduled my appearance.

I spent the next week writing my five-minute set. I would open with a joke about Mississippi. I wasn't proud about throwing my home state under the bus, but it was low hanging fruit and I thought it was funny, so I went with it. I rehearsed my set the following week until I could recite it in my sleep. One of the biggest fears of a beginning comic is forgetting your material. This doesn't happen when you become a professional because you've done it so much you can easily get back on track if you find yourself daydreaming on stage. I wasn't a professional, though, and the fear was real. Forgetting my material wasn't my only fear. As that Saturday grew closer, I was starting to freak out at the thought of going on stage in front of a group of strangers. By the day of the show, I was sick to my stomach.

When I woke up on the day of the show, I was a mess. I would rather have swam through a river filled with starving crocodiles than do what I was about to do. It was too late, though. I decided I was going to be a comedian and this was just something I was going to have to deal with, so we headed to Hoover. We checked into our hotel, and I had a cup of coffee before I left for the club. My hand was shaking so bad the coffee was spilling out of the cup. I also looked like I had seen a ghost. My wife later told me that she started crying after I left the hotel because I looked so pitiful.

I pulled out of the hotel and started driving to the club. I came to a red light at the end of the road. Standing in the middle of the intersection was a very large Hoover police officer who was sweating profusely, and he didn't look like he was in a good mood. Whatever I did obviously made his mood worse because he screamed at the top of his lungs for me to go in a direction I didn't want to go. This was not the reception to Hoover, Alabama I was hoping for. I followed his directions and found an alternate route to the club.

I walked into the club and headed back to the room where the open mic was held. The woman running the show explained how everything would work and that I would be going up third. I went back out to the bar to get something to drink. I stared at the liquor bottles behind the bar and considered my options. Do I start chugging whiskey to get my courage up or get a Sprite and do this like a man? I got the Sprite. I went back into the room as the show was about to begin. The room was packed with about one hundred people. I stood backstage sipping my Sprite as the first two people did their set. I was surprisingly calm.

The woman running the show said I was up next, so I stepped to the curtain leading to the stage. The sound guy looked to see if I was ready, and I nodded yes. He said, "Please welcome Pat McCool." I stepped onto the stage, and it felt like I was having an out-of-body experience. I could hear John Cougar's "Jack and Diane" blaring from the speakers, and somebody yelled, "Yeah Pat!" As far as I knew, I didn't know anybody from Hoover, but I appreciated the support. As I stepped to the microphone, I could feel my legs shaking. The lights were so bright I couldn't see anything. It was like I could have seen dead family members if I looked at them long enough. I did my first joke. The room exploded! I did my second, and they exploded again. They laughed hysterically at my whole five minute set, and I floated off the stage.

I walked backstage, and the woman who ran the show looked at me and said, "Wow, how long have you been doing comedy?"

I said, "Five minutes."

"Well you should keep doing it."

I sat backstage to listen to the next two guys. I wanted to see if the crowd responded to them the same way they responded to me. They didn't. Both of the guys stunk the place up. I hate say it, but I was thrilled. I thanked the woman for having me and bolted out of the club to call Gwen. She answered the phone, and I yelled, "I did it! I freaking did it!" It was the best feeling of my life. I had confronted my demons and punched them in the face. There would be plenty of nights in my comedy career that wouldn't go as well as that one, but from that point forward, I knew I could stand on stage and make people laugh.

I went back two weeks later with five minutes of new material. The owner of the club, Bruce Ayers, who is one of the best guys in the business, watched me this time. After the show, he invited me into his office. He said I had great stage presence and I could be good at this if I worked at it. I asked him what he meant by great stage presence, and he said I looked relaxed, like I wasn't nervous. This was news to me because my legs felt like spaghetti the whole time I was up there, but obviously nobody could tell. He gave me some advice on the business and encouraged me to keep at it. Even though I didn't want to hear some of it, everything he told me to expect turned out to be true. I have always appreciated that he took the time to help me out.

I went to a few more open mics before approaching Bruce about booking me on the main stage. The open mic was in the Broadway room where private parties were held, and it seated about one hundred people. The main room in the Stardome seated over five hundred and is one of the best comedy clubs in the country. Bruce told me I wasn't ready yet. He explained there was an ocean of difference between five minutes at an open mic and performing in front of a real crowd at a comedy club. I didn't believe him. I was killing at the open mic and was certain I would do the same on a real stage if given the chance.

So he asked his stepdaughter, who did the booking for the Stardome, to make some calls for me. A few days later, I got a call from a guy in North Carolina who booked shows around the south. He offered me an MC gig in a small town in Georgia. Bruce explained to me that doing MC gigs was the way to develop your act until you were ready to be a feature or headliner. A typical comedy show has three acts. The MC does fifteen minutes, the feature does thirty, and the headliner does between forty-five and sixty.

There is a big difference between being an MC and a feature or headliner. An MC's job is to get the crowd laughing, make whatever announcements the club wants, and properly introduce the other two acts. You don't even have to do a full fifteen minutes as long as you can get the crowd laughing and run the show properly. It's far more important not to go over fifteen minutes than it is to go under. The best way to get on the bad side of a feature or headlining comedian is to go over your time and you don't want to do that. The most important people in helping you climb the comedy ladder are other comedians. This wasn't going to be a problem for me because I only had twelve minutes of material that I was hanging onto like a life raft.

I was sick the week leading up to the show. Not nervous sick but a pain in my abdomen that was getting worse each day. Gwen went with me and would wait at the hotel. By the time we got there, I could barely walk. We got to our room, and I sat down in so much pain I didn't know if I was going to be able to get up. When the time came to leave for the show, the pain miraculously disappeared. Somehow I was able to go do the show without the slightest discomfort. Everything went well except for me butchering the feature act's introduction, which he had written on a napkin. He wouldn't be giving me any recommendations, but I made the crowd laugh and ran the show well. Most importantly, I got paid for standing on stage and making people laugh.

When I got back to the hotel, the pain returned. I collapsed on the bed, started shaking uncontrollably, and broke out in a cold sweat. The next morning, Gwen drove home and took me straight to the emergency room. I had a 103 degree temperature, and they admitted me immediately. When the tests came back, they revealed I had a severe case of diverticulitis. The doctor said he couldn't believe I was able to walk and if I had waited much longer I could have died from it. I spent a week in the hospital. The doctor wanted to take a nice chunk of my lower intestine out. I asked him if that was really necessary. He said no, but since I had met my deductible, now would be a great time to do it. Maybe I'm crazy but I didn't think having met my deductible was a good enough reason for slicing my stomach open. I opted instead to increase my daily fiber intake.

Apparently, I had done well enough at the MC gig for the booker to offer me a feature spot a few weeks later. Going from being an MC to a feature act after one show was a big deal. All I needed was to be able to make people laugh for thirty minutes. I couldn't, but I wasn't going to let that stop me. I accepted the gig and wrote fifteen minutes of new material and added it to my set. I was about to find out that just because you wrote fifteen minutes of material didn't mean you had fifteen minutes. In comedy, you don't know if something's funny until you walk on stage and try it out. You're not performing in front of your mom or at the office water cooler where your coworkers give you a courtesy laugh so they won't hurt your feelings.

I drove to Bainbridge, Georgia where the show was being held and pulled up to the venue. It was a hotel that was having a comedy night in their restaurant. Performing at a comedy night is different than a comedy club. A comedy club is set up for comedy with a professional sound and light system. It's also run by people who know what they're doing. I'm not saying all comedy nights are run by people who don't know what they're doing, but some are better at it than others. This comedy night was being run by the others.

I had talked to the guy running the show a couple of days earlier, and he told me they put out a few thousand fliers that week, so he was expecting a big crowd. When I got to the entrance of the restaurant where the show was being held, I noticed a table sitting by the door. On that table was a stack of three thousand fliers. Apparently his idea of promotion was giving a flier to people after they got to the show. I realized at that point the prospect of a big crowd was iffy at best.

The next sign of trouble was the large half-exposed rear end attached to the guy installing the lights. I had seen this on plumbers in my kitchen before, but not on a guy setting up the lighting for a comedy show. It wasn't so much his exposed derriere that got my attention as it was his idea of a spotlight for a comedy show. He was installing the floodlights from his pickup truck that he used for hunting, both of them. When I walked on stage, I could feel my skin sizzling. I now knew what food at a buffet felt like.

If fifteen people was the promoter's idea of a big crowd, he would have been right. That went down to fourteen during the show because one woman had to leave because her husband got arrested for driving with a suspended license. My set actually went well. Half of the new material worked, and I just moved quickly through the stuff that didn't. This would turn out to be the way I would handle trying out new material to this day. If people don't laugh at a joke, just move along like it wasn't supposed to be funny in the first place. The lesson I learned that night was not to try so much new material at one time. Going from a funny joke, to a not funny one, back to a funny one is okay. Going from a not funny one, to a not funny one, back to a not funny one can get a little awkward.

Fortunately, things didn't get awkward for me and I had a great set even though it only lasted twenty minutes. That wasn't a problem though because I was working with Roy Wood Jr., a great guy and really funny comic who now has his own sitcom on TV. He did an extra ten minutes to cover my time and had no problem helping me out. The small crowd turned out to be helpful too because if you're going to be a comic, you're going to perform in front of small crowds. The sooner you learn how to do it, the better.

The guy booked me in another show a few weeks later. It was a couple of hours down the road from the last one, which was an hour or two down the road from the first one. I was working my way down a stretch of highway in southern Georgia, gaining fans from town to town, but I would leave the next town with the same amount of fans

I showed up with. This was Valdosta, Georgia, which I'm sure is a great southern town filled with wonderful people. For me, however, just hearing the name makes me want to curl up under a blanket.

The guy who was headlining called me the day before the show and asked if I could give him a ride. He was in Atlanta, and I was in Hattiesburg. I would have to drive over two hundred miles to pick him up and assumed he would understand why I couldn't. I assumed wrong. He thought it should be no problem for me to leave three hours early and drive to Atlanta, then another three hours to Valdosta. When I got off the phone, it was obvious I wasn't going to be working with someone like Roy Wood Jr.

Gwen was with me on this trip. She was going to wait at the hotel while I went to the show. The hotel was a fine establishment called the Holly. The first disconcerting sign was the people hanging out in the parking lot. People hanging out in a hotel parking lot is never a good sign. I went into the office and got the room key. It was actually a key, not a key card. It had been a while since I had stayed in a hotel with an actual key, but as long as it opened the door, I was good with it. The room was about what I expected when I got the key, small and dingy. We were only going to be there one night, so we settled in and I headed for the show.

I arrived at the bar where the show was held and looked for my contact person. After about fifteen minutes, a distressed-looking girl showed up and the first thing she asked me was, "How much time can you do?" This was the last thing I wanted to be asked. I had planned on doing the twenty-three minutes that worked the last time, then winging the final seven. In comedy, if winging it is part of your plan, then you don't have a plan. As it turned out, I wasn't just seven minutes short of material. I was an hour short of material because she asked if I could do the whole show myself. I asked how much time the MC could do. She said there wasn't an MC.

I realized right then that this was a time for honesty and assured her that I could not do the whole show myself. I asked her what happened to the headliner. She said he was in town but refusing to do the show because he thought he was getting paid in cash but the bar was paying with a check. Since I wouldn't drive three hours out of my way to pick him up, he had another guy drive him down and had promised to give him money for the ride after he got paid. She said she was going to call the booker to see what they could work out and to hang around and see what they were going to do.

I called Gwen to explain what was happening and see how she was doing at the hotel. She said she was worried because there seemed to be a fight going on in the room next to ours. She said people were screaming and she had just heard what sounded like a piece of furniture hit the wall. I didn't know who was in the most peril, me or her. It was me. The brawling people in the next room were the headliner and the guy he bummed a ride from. I would have been perfectly happy at this point if they had just canceled the whole thing.

That didn't happen. The girl came back and said they had worked something out with the brawling headliner. She introduced me to the guy who was running the sound and said we would go ahead and start the show. I gave my introduction to the sound guy, and he gave me a puzzled look. He asked me what this was, and I told him it was how I wanted to be introduced. He said he wasn't planning on introducing anybody, he was just there to run the sound. I talked him into at least going on stage and telling everybody to take a seat then announcing my name.

I wasn't as concerned with him announcing my name as I was him telling everybody to take a seat. The place was full of people, but they didn't seem to be there for a comedy show. It was a typical bar scene where everyone was there to either get intoxicated or pick up girls. The sound guy walked on stage and asked everybody to quiet down and take a seat. Nobody listened. He asked louder the second time. They didn't listen again. The third time he screamed as loud as he could with the same results. He just looked at me with his hands in the air and shook his head like he had done all he could. He then put the microphone in the stand and screamed, "Good luck." I needed more than luck.

This crowd wasn't sitting down and being quiet because they weren't there for a comedy show. I took the stage and started plowing through my set even though nobody was paying attention. To make matters worse, my twenty-three minutes was turning into fifteen because other than the occasional drunk guy turning to me and screaming "Lynyrd Skynyrd," nobody was responding at all. You learn quickly in comedy that thirty minutes can turn into twenty if nobody is laughing, and nobody was laughing.

I did have one moment where I thought I might have won the crowd over. In the middle of a joke, half of the crowd looked towards me and started cheering wildly. I paused for a second to see if they were cheering me for some inexplicable reason, or was something going on behind me. Something was going on behind me. There was a big screen TV on the wall behind the stage, and it was showing the Atlanta Braves baseball game. Chipper Jones had just hit a grand slam.

My set finally came to a merciful end, and I thanked the crowd for nothing just as the ride-bumming headliner walked in. I didn't stick around. I went back to the hotel to patch myself up. When I got back to the hotel and calmed down, I started thinking that maybe Bruce Ayers was right after all. He was right of course, but if I was going to be a stand-up comedian, I was going to have to do comedy nights. If I was going to do comedy nights, I was going to perform at places like this, but next time I would be ready for it.

I got ready by doing what Bruce had suggested in the first place. I got a week long MC gig at a comedy club and worked on my act. I called Julie Jusmore, the booker for the Comedy House Theater Comedy Clubs, and talked her into booking me at one of her clubs. I had to talk her into it because the demo tape I sent her only showed me from the neck down. Since she wasn't in the market for a headless comedian, I had to convince her over the phone I could do it. I had to wear her out by calling every few days, but she finally rewarded my tenacity by booking me for a week at their club in Columbia, South Carolina.

The week went great, and she invited me back. Not only did Julie invite me back, but I also worked with two great guys who offered to help me out. One of the guys was Jim Holder, who was very complimentary of my act and gave me the name of a booking agent to call. He told me I was as good as anybody the booking agent had working for him. The people who ran the club also told me if I wanted to do the feature spot to tell Julie and they would give me a recommendation. This was just what I needed.

CHAPTER 19

DON'T STARE AT THE CELEBRITIES

The booking agent Jim Holder hooked me up with gave me gigs in places like Texarkana, Texas; Cape Girardeau, Missouri; and Terre Haute, Indiana. They weren't gigs at A clubs, but I was getting better and learning what road comedy was about. What road comedy was about at that point for me was a lot of driving and staying in places I would not set foot in if I had the choice. One of those was in Mountain Home, Arkansas. The "resort" hotel I was supposed to stay in had been foreclosed on the week before. The coat hanger antenna on the TV and the bathroom door hanging off the wall didn't make it any more comforting. I figured it was only one night and I wasn't there for a four-star vacation, so I decided I would stay there without whining about it. Until the snake slithered under the back door. Then it was time to whine. Snakes slithering under back doors are game changers for me. I rented a room at a hotel and paid for it myself.

I eventually got an opportunity to perform at the Hollywood Improv in Los Angeles. This was the holy grail of comedy to me. I had watched A&E's *An Evening at the Improv* religiously in the 1980s and almost every well-known comedian had been on it. Gwen flew out with me, and we stayed at the Hyatt on Sunset Boulevard. I was familiar with this hotel because a comedian had jumped to his death there ten years earlier. I remember checking in and noticing the guy at the desk was being really friendly. He asked if I was from Colorado for some reason. When I told him I was from Mississippi, he wasn't being friendly anymore.

I drove to the Improv the next night and pulled in the parking lot behind Fred Segal. It's a store where you will see a lot of celebrities shopping. I wasn't a celebrity but I was parking my rental car there anyway. I walked into the club and found the woman who was running the show. She gave me my spot in the lineup and told me we would be starting in thirty minutes. I didn't have to worry about getting nervous during that thirty minutes because I was already a train wreck. I was getting over my stage fright with experience but this was the Improv.

She announced the show was starting, and I walked into the hallway leading to the showroom. There is no green room at the Improv. You just stand in the hallway and try to stay out of everybody's way until your name is called. I couldn't help thinking about all of the well-known comedians who stood in that hallway dodging waitresses during the filming of *Evening at the Improv*. As the show started, I slipped into the showroom and leaned against the wall. I wanted to see what kind of reaction the comics before me were getting. This was a showcase, so everyone was doing seven minutes. I was seventh in the lineup, so it would be a few minutes before it was my time to go up. I watched the first three comics and they all did okay, but nobody set the room on fire. I then stepped back into the hallway to wait my turn.

Finally, the sixth comic in the lineup was wrapping up her set, so I stepped back into the room. The MC whom I had never met introduced me like she had known me all her life, and I took the stage. I did my first bit, and the crowd erupted. I did my second bit, and they erupted again. I breathed and they erupted. My whole set went like that, and I walked off the stage to cheers, applause, and high fives. I was elated as I walked out of the door. I expected it to go well, and it wasn't the first time a crowd had reacted like that, but that was more than I had hoped for.

I went outside to call Gwen and give her the news. I was really excited. I didn't want anybody thinking I was some idiot from Mississippi who just had his first great set at the Improv, which I was, so I crouched beside a car and excitedly whispered the news to Gwen. While I was telling her how awesome her husband was, a lady walked up and looked at me like I was trying to break into her Porsche. Obviously she didn't know who I was, but I got away from her car before she called the police.

I walked back to the entrance to the club and started talking to Vito, the doorman. A minute later, a woman and a man holding a box of files walked out. The woman looked at me excitedly and said, "You were fantastic," and then asked me my name. She told me her name and dipped her sunglasses like I should know who she was. She said she was a casting director and presently casting a movie with Antonio Banderas in South America. She introduced me to the guy with the box and said he was in the movie business too. He told me I was the most original comedian he'd ever seen and watching me was like having someone stand in their living room talking to them.

A few more people walked past and complimented me. Vito the doorman was watching this and said, "Man this is awesome. I need to introduce you to Matt." Matt was managing the Improv at the time. He walked out a couple of minutes later and started talking to a girl on the sidewalk. Vito and I overheard him ask her if she had seen anyone she liked. She pointed to me and said, "The guy from Tennessee was really funny." People still occasionally refer to me as the guy from Tennessee. I guess they think it's close enough. She then walked over and introduced herself. She was scouting for a talent agency and asked me if I lived in LA. I told her I still lived in Mississippi. She gave me her card and told me to let her know when I was back in town.

Vito took me over and introduced me to Matt, who hadn't seen the show. Vito told him what all the people had said and encouraged him to give me regular bookings at the club. We talked for a few minutes, and Matt gave me his phone number and told me to call him. He said I would have to do a showcase with Stu, who booked the club. I didn't understand why I needed to do a showcase when I had just done a showcase, but I obviously needed to do one while Stu was watching. Either way, I had the chance to perform regularly at the Hollywood Improv and was convinced I was fifteen minutes away from fame and fortune. I was wrong, but I would be coming back to LA.

I went back to the hotel and picked Gwen up to go to dinner and celebrate. We went to Loiuse's Trattoria on Sunset. We were eating outside on the patio, and while we were waiting on our food, I thought I noticed Garry Marshall sitting inside. I got up to go to the restroom to see if it was him. Gwen warned me not to make a fool of myself, but it was a warning I had ignored many times in the past. As I walked out of the bathroom, I looked over and could clearly see that it was him. Just to make sure, I kept looking.

Apparently, there is some rule in Hollywood that you're not supposed to stare at celebrities. The more I stared, the bigger his eyes got until he reached the point where I thought he was about to get up and take a swing at me. I quickly employed the tactic I had used in the past when a girl thought I was staring at her. I would look past them and act like I was more interested in what was behind them. The problem was there was a blank wall behind him, so I walked the length of the restaurant staring at a blank wall like I was amazed by it.

Gwen watched this through the window, and when I got back to the table, she said, "You just couldn't help yourself, could you?" Of course I couldn't help myself, but I didn't care. I figured it was just a matter of time before he knew who I was anyway.

I called every week for the next four weeks until Stu scheduled his next showcase. It would be a month later, which was two months since my last appearance. Two months is a lifetime in Hollywood. People will forget about you by the end of the week much less two months. I flew out to do the showcase, and when I got to the club, I realized this would be different from the last one. There wouldn't be a real audience, just a bunch of other comics auditioning for Stu. Showcases with only comics in the audience are horrible. You either have the small group of supportive nice guys that laugh at everything or the guys that stare at you like they want to beat you to a pulp. This crowd seemed to be made up of the last group. It didn't matter though. The only person that I needed to laugh was Stu, and he did. He actually apologized after the show for making me audition and said I was in.

It would be two more months before I could go back. We still lived in Mississippi and had plans to move to Los Angeles, but we still had kids in school. We felt like we couldn't move from Hattiesburg until they were older. I booked a hotel for the week and flew out to do my next set. I didn't know what night I would perform because you couldn't just schedule a specific night. The way it worked was, you called at the beginning of the week and gave Stu the nights you would be available. He would then let you know what night or nights you'd be in the lineup. I couldn't just fly in one day and out the next. I had to pay for a hotel room for four nights just to get twenty minutes on stage. It was expensive, but I did it anyway.

I showed up at the club a few minutes before the show started, and the person running it gave me my slot in the lineup. She also told me that it could change because Jerry Seinfeld was stopping in for a set. When somebody like Seinfeld comes in, they put him right up. He doesn't have to stand around sipping Perrier checking the piece of paper on the wall for his time slot. A lot of people, especially tourists, go to clubs like the Improv hoping they will see somebody famous and there's always a chance they will. This is where guys like Seinfeld work out their material. He'll do twenty minutes at the Improv then drive around to the Laugh Factory on Sunset and do twenty more.

My spot was early in the lineup and my set went great. Not like it did the first time when I felt like I owned the place, but I was really happy with it. When I finished, I stayed in the showroom to see if Seinfeld was coming anytime soon. After the next comic finished, I noticed two people step into the room. One was Jerry and he was standing next to me. He did his set, talked to the crowd a minute, and walked out of the door. I, of course, followed. When I got outside, I saw him and another guy talking to each other with no one else around. I was surprised there wasn't a crowd of people trying to talk to him. I was obviously the only person in West Hollywood that didn't know you weren't supposed to hassle celebrities.

So I walked over to speak with him. He was talking to George Shapiro, who was Seinfeld's manager and one of the most well-known people in the entertainment business. He had also been Andy Kaufman's manager and was one of the main reasons for his success. He was played by Danny Devito in the movie *The Man in the Moon*, although he looks nothing like him. So there I was, just like I had envisioned, me, Jerry, and George standing out in front of the Improv shooting the breeze. Except we weren't shooting the breeze. I was asking Jerry to sign my head shot. I don't know what prompted me to do that, but I wanted to speak with him and couldn't just say, "Hey, man, how's the family?" He was actually very nice about it, and Shapiro helped by holding my picture while Jerry signed it because he had a bottle in his other hand.

I thanked him and stepped back over to the edge of the sidewalk where I was acting like I was waiting for a ride. I wasn't waiting for a ride because I had a rental car parked behind Fred Segal. It wasn't just any rental car either. It was the cheapest thing Fox Rent-A-Car had. I don't think they even sold them in America. It was so small I could wave out of the back window while I was driving. I could barely close the hatch with my suitcase in the back. I would try to be as inconspicuous as possible when I pulled up next to the Lamborghinis and Bentleys at the intersection of La Cienaga and Sunset Boulevard.

I began regretting my decision to save a few bucks on a rental car when Seinfeld started to leave. He got in a vintage Porsche that was parked in front of the club. He couldn't get it to start. He tried again, and it still wouldn't start. Being an opportunist, I immediately thought that I could give him a ride to wherever he needed to go that night and become best buddies along the way. Then I remembered the chick magnet I had parked behind Fred Segal and just couldn't envision tooling Jerry around Hollywood with his head sticking out of the window. It didn't matter anyway, as on the third try his car started and he sped down Melrose Avenue.

I would make several more trips to Los Angeles to do sets at the Improv. On my last trip, I began to realize this was getting me nowhere. This wasn't the eighties anymore. In the eighties, if you had an original act, you could get noticed at places like the Improv or Comedy Store and land a TV deal for your own sitcom. That had become my plan after my initial appearance at the Improv. I was about twenty years too late. Except for the occasional showcase, nobody from the entertainment industry was going to comedy clubs.

Doing twenty minute sets every four or five months was wasting my time and money. I decided I wasn't coming back to LA until I could live there.

On my last trip to the Improv, I sat at the bar for a while after my set. This is what I typically did. I had met some other comics and gained some insight into the business. You can learn a lot about the comedy business by hanging out with comedians. Nobody I knew was there that night, so after about an hour, I got ready to leave.

Just before I got up, a friendly guy with a New York accent who had just finished his set sat down and said hello. We struck up a conversation and hit it off immediately. He was a former New York City firefighter who lost a lot of friends in the 9-11 attack on the World Trade Center. He started doing comedy not long after that and won the funniest fireman contest that was held by a network TV show. He started an organization that did comedy shows dedicated to helping firefighters, police officers etc., and their families. When I got ready to leave, he told me to look him up if I ever came to New York City. I didn't realize it at the time, but my last visit to the Improv would have a far greater impact on my life than my first.

CHAPTER 20

SOMEONE GAINED,
SOMEONE LOST

A few weeks later, I was back at the Comedy House Theater in Columbia, South Carolina. On the first night of the week long gig, I was getting ready to go on stage. The headliner hadn't shown up, and everyone was starting to get a little nervous. Just before I went on stage, a guy named Joey, who looked like he was straight from Central Casting, walked into the green room. He wore a small rimmed black hat, tuxedo shirt, and black vest with matching pants. He greeted me in a thick Brooklyn accent with, "Hey, hey, hey, how ya doin'?" I introduced myself and headed for the stage.

After my set, I stayed to watch him. The beginning of his act was set to music, and he came out wearing a *Phantom of the Opera* mask and immediately lit his hands on fire. He then started speaking in Italian, then did magic, then stand-up comedy, then went out into the audience, and finally pulled a series of puppets out and brought the house down. I had never seen anything like it, nor had I ever seen anybody like him.

I was waiting for him in the green room to compliment him on his act after he finished. He walked in, his clothes drenched in sweat, and said, "Good job, puppy, let's talk when you get the chance." We had plenty of chances to talk that week, and by the time we had finished talking, I was planning on flying to New York and going out on the road with him. He told me my act would go over great in the

New York area and if I went on the road with him it would change my life. He was right. I just didn't know how right he was.

A month later, I flew into Newark Liberty Airport on Joey's birthday. He was from Brooklyn but now lived in Central New Jersey with his wife and kids. Ironically, we were going to drive back to the south for a two-week run of shows. I walked out of the airport and waited for him to show up. A few minutes later, I saw him coming. He was in a silver Mercedes SUV flying around the corner, weaving through traffic and honking at people. At first this made me nervous, but I would later discover that everybody in New Jersey drove like this. Even nuns will honk at you in New Jersey.

I jumped in, and we took off. We got back to his house where they were finishing his birthday celebration. We ate dinner and then went to sleep to rest up for the long trip. Forty-five minutes later, he woke me up and said it's time to go. I hadn't been this rattled since my first morning in basic training where a drill sergeant woke me up by yanking the blanket off me at five o'clock. After forty-five minutes of sleep, we were now going to make a thirteen-hour drive to Knoxville, Tennessee. I figured it was okay because one of the reasons I had flown to New Jersey was so we could share the driving and I could rest while he took his turn.

Then I learned his idea of taking turns driving. We left his house, drove to the highway, and stopped at the first gas station. He went inside and got each of us a cup of coffee. Then he came back to the car and said, "You want to drive for a while?" I had no idea "drive for a while" meant until we were thirty miles from Knoxville. To make matters worse, we weren't carrying ordinary cargo. In the back of his SUV he had rabbits, birds, flammable liquids, and a huge box that he used to saw people in half. I drove into Pennsylvania listening to doves flap their wings every time I hit a bump wondering how in the world I had ended up where I was.

We arrived in Knoxville about an hour before the show started. We checked into our hotel, which was next door to the Knoxville Comedy Zone, where we would be performing for the next five days. By the time the show started, I had been awake for over thirty-six hours with the exception of the forty-five minutes of sleep at Joey's house. I forgot half of my act and only did about fifteen minutes. I didn't actually forget my material. I was just too sleepy to realize I had skipped part of it when I got to the end of my set. This wasn't a problem though, because Joey covered the time without thinking twice about it. He was the best club entertainer I had seen, and working with him would be a great way to build my act.

After the show that night, I was ready to go to my room and slip into a self-induced coma. Joey, on the other hand, actually wanted to head out on the town. It wasn't just because he was well rested from the ride down either. He always had to be doing something, whether it was going to a bar at one o'clock in the morning or breakfast at six o'clock. He was like the Energizer bunny on steroids. This was a problem for me because I was the exact opposite. I wanted to take care of my business and go back to my room and watch something riveting like the history of concrete on the History Channel. This would become a daily battle. He would take the Do Not Disturb sign off my door and drop it on the ground so he could pound on my door at all hours of the day and night. I thought my job was to stand on stage and entertain an audience for thirty minutes. Joey thought my job was to entertain him twenty-four hours a day.

I had a great week in Knoxville. It was a great club, and I became friends with some of the staff. The most important thing was, I had done well at a Comedy Zone. The Comedy Zone clubs are run by an agency out of Charlotte, North Carolina, and they are the top booking agency in the south and eastern part of the country. We did two more comedy nights the following week before wrapping up the trip at another Comedy Zone in Johnson City, Tennessee. I volunteered to drive us back to New Jersey because riding in the car while Joey drove was akin to being on a boat being tossed by large waves. He would put his foot on the gas pedal and then take it off, then jerk the steering wheel and do it again. He did this from one end of Tennessee to the other until I realized I would either have to drive or stop and throw up every sixty miles. He dropped me off at the airport in New Jersey. I gave him a hug and said, "I'll see you soon," but I had *no* intention of ever getting in the car with that fool again.

A month later, we're driving from Atlanta to Columbus, Georgia. I think my relationship with Joey became like one with an abusive spouse. You think they might kill you but for some reason you keep going back. I wouldn't lose my life on this trip, but it would definitely be changed. We did one night in Columbus and then the following night in Cordele. Cordele was interesting because it was the first time I had done comedy with a thirty-mile-an-hour wind blowing in my face. Apparently, somebody thought it would be a good idea to have the show at the edge of a lake. It's never a good idea to have a comedy show at the edge of a lake, or anywhere outside. I almost lost my voice screaming at the audience who were more concerned with keeping their chicken fingers and cheese sticks from blowing off the table than listening to me.

We roll into Pineville, North Carolina on a Friday for a weekend of shows at the Pineville Diner Theater. Pineville is a suburb of Charlotte. I had never been to Charlotte, but it would be a place that Gwen and I would come to know well. After my set the first night, I sat down at the bar and started talking to the bartender. I noticed one of the waitresses sitting at the end of the bar. She had a tired and almost sad look on her face. She glanced at me, and I asked her how she was doing. She said she was fine in a heavy eastern European accent and asked how I was doing. Noticing her accent, I asked where she was from.

She said, "I am from Ukraine."

This peaked my interest because while I had traveled a lot in my life, I was from south Mississippi and had never met anyone from Eastern Europe. For the twenty-two years my dad spent in the army, the Soviet Bloc countries, which Ukraine was a part of, were our mortal enemies. I had also spent a summer at Fort Sill, Oklahoma training to kill people from countries like Ukraine. I couldn't help thinking as I looked at this girl how someone like this had ever been my enemy. I was interested in what life was like in Ukraine now that the Iron Curtain had come down, so I asked her. She started telling me a story that broke my heart.

I won't go into details about the story she told me, but life in her country was bad enough for her to leave her family and travel to a place she had never been on the other side of the world. I thought about my own daughters and how heart-wrenching it would be if they had to do something like that just to have the opportunity to pursue a life of happiness and prosperity. We talked for a while, and before I got up to leave, I asked the bartender if what she had told me was true. She assured me it was. I stepped over, shook her hand and said, "My name is Pat." She said, "My name is Kseniia, nice talking to you."

I went back to my hotel and called Gwen like I would typically do. I told her about this kid I had met and the story she told me. Gwen said she would pray for her and we said good-bye. That's what Gwen did. She prayed for everybody. She prayed for the homeless guy on the corner (after giving him twenty dollars), the UPS driver, the yard man, and the cat across the street. If she thought you were in need, she prayed for you. If you weren't, she prayed for you anyway. I had seen crazy things happen when Gwen started praying for somebody and crazy things were about to happen now.

I stayed in touch with Kseniia after I left Charlotte, and Gwen started communicating with her too. Gwen learned everything she could about the country of Ukraine and had the Ukrainian national anthem as the ring tone on her phone. She prayed for her every day along with the other two hundred people and animals she had on her prayer list. A few months later, I was in Macon, Georgia, performing at the Whiskey River Comedy Club. The phone rang early in the morning, and it was an excited Kseniia on the other end. It was her birthday, and she had awoken to find a large box on her doorstep. Gwen had sent her a birthday box filled with presents and money. She thanked me over and over and said, "This is like a real birthday." Well, it was her birthday and she deserved to have a real one, and Gwen made sure she did.

Gwen and I visited Kseniia in Charlotte not long after that, and she became part of our family. She calls Gwen her "Chicken Mama." She was trying to refer to her as a mother hen one time, but it came out that way and the name stuck. We visited her every chance we could, and one time in particular stands out. It was Fourth of July. We had a cookout at Kseniia's apartment, and she invited all her friends over, some of which we already knew. One of those was a Russian guy named Alexei. He was a former KGB officer. The other people at the cookout were all either from Russia or former Soviet Bloc countries. I couldn't help but be amused as they chided me for not getting into the spirit of Independence Day. They told me it wasn't just a time to eat hot dogs, but a time to celebrate how great our country of America is.

Every ten minutes they would hold up their glass, and say, "Independence!" That was the best Fourth of July of my life. I spent it saluting independence with a former KGB agent who I had spent half of my life wanting to kill. I learned a valuable lesson that day, that people all over the world are the same. They just want the opportunity to live their lives in peace and pursue happiness for them and their families.

Kseniia went on to graduate with honors from Belk Business School at the University of North Carolina Charlotte. Gwen and I were there to watch her receive her diploma with tears in our eyes. She met a great guy named Brian and married him a couple of years later. They live in Charlotte and both have great careers. They also just welcomed their first child into the world, Julliete Isabella "Jules" Anderson. Her mother, who had to watch her eighteen-year-old daughter leave home and not know what was happening to her for years, is now able to visit her often.

Kseniia is one of mine and Gwen's great inspirations. She left home as a child determined to have the life she wanted. She worked three jobs at one time. I spoke with her one day after she had worked over twenty-two hours straight. She saved money for school and sent what she had left back to her family. She told me something one day that I never forgot. She said, "Pat, when things get tough and I don't want to go on, I just focus on the next thing I have to do." That has come in handy for me in times when I found myself in the same situation. Kind of ironic, I thought. God put me in her life to inspire her, but it turned out to be the other way around.

When Joey and I left Charlotte on Sunday after our two nights in Pineville, I had him drop me off at the airport. We still had two weeks of a month-long road trip left, but our next show wasn't until

Thursday, so we had three days to kill. I wasn't about to spend it entertaining him, so I was flying home to see Gwen, then flying back to meet him in Charleston, West Virginia where our next show was. He wasn't happy about it either. God forbid, he would have to amuse himself for three whole days. He had told everybody at the Pineville Theater who would listen how bad I was treating him. I remember hearing him tell the busboy, "He's flying home on Sunday and I have to pick him up at the airport in Charleston. Isn't that crazy!?" Nobody thought it was crazy. They had all spent two days with him and perfectly understood.

When Joey came to pick me up at the airport, I began to think maybe I should have stayed with him. I saw his car coming up the hill outside of baggage claim, and it looked like no one was driving it. He had either spent the whole time drinking or hadn't gone to sleep at all because he was slumped over in the driver's seat with one hand on the steering wheel half asleep. As the car topped the hill where I was waiting, he opened the door and rolled out to get in the passenger seat so I could drive. The only problem was, he didn't put the car in park. I screamed at the top of my lungs as the car started rolling down the hill towards pedestrians. He didn't hear me, so I took off running as fast as I could. I caught up to it, jumped in, and stopped it just before it slammed into a hotel shuttle bus full of people.

We were at each other's throats that night as the show was beginning. He was mad I had left him to fend for himself while I went home, and I was mad that he was mad about it. It wasn't uncommon for us to argue, but the show was about to start and there would be a better time to sort this out. He wanted to discuss it right then, but the MC was calling me to the stage. I heard his voice over Joey, yelling, "And he's opened for Jerry Seinfeld, from Mississippi, please welcome Pat McCool."

I hadn't opened for Seinfeld of course, but I had technically "worked" with Seinfeld and that's what I had told an MC a few months back. That MC wrote on a napkin "opened for" instead of "worked with," and when he announced me that way, some people in the audience said, "Oooohhh." It obviously sounded impressive, so I took the napkin from the MC after the show. From then on, when an

MC asked me how I wanted to be introduced, I just handed him the napkin and said, "You can just use what the last guy used." I never told anybody that I had opened for Seinfeld, so I wasn't being dishonest and there was no way Gwen could call me on the carpet for it.

When I returned home from our month-long run of shows, I had begun the process of adding a now beloved member to our family. Tragically, fate had begun the process of taking one away. It would be the worst time of my wife's life. I mentioned earlier in this book that life-changing events don't usually happen at planned times; they happen on random weekdays in the middle of the afternoon. A few weeks after I returned, Gwen and I both came down with a bad case of the flu. It was so bad I lay in the bed for days. Gwen was just as sick, but she never lay in the bed. She's the toughest person I have ever known. No matter how sick she was, she went on with life and took care of whatever and whomever she had to take care of.

One afternoon, I woke up and walked into the kitchen to get something to drink. I can still clearly remember her face as she stopped me in the hallway and said, "Leo has cancer." Leo was Gwen's brother and one of the nicest guys I've ever met. You could say the same about Gwen's whole family. They love and support each other like no family I know. If somebody is down, they rally around them. If somebody's in need, they come to their aid. They make the well-being of those they love their business. They had already lost James, Gwen's sister Beki's husband, to cancer and were determined not to lose Leo, but they were in for the fight of their lives.

Gwen and Leo were especially close. Leo had gone through a divorce and would call Gwen for advice on everything from women to fashion. He, like me before I met Gwen, needed all the fashion help he could get. It wasn't uncommon for Leo to show up with his shirt tucked into blue jean shorts with a cell phone holder attached to his belt. He would round that off with sandals and white socks with stripes on the top. Regardless of his fashion shortcomings, Leo was a special guy. He never had a bad word to say about anybody, and people just liked being around him.

Leo's battle was one that I'm sure is familiar to many families. You have days you're convinced they're going to make it and days you're not so sure. You keep praying and believing. When that doesn't work, you do it some more. You cry out to God and don't understand why this is happening. You do everything you can until you reach the point you can do no more. That point came. Leo lost his battle and went to wait on his family in heaven. I have never seen my wife hurt so badly. It's a helpless feeling to watch the person you have dedicated your life to protecting suffer, and there is nothing you can do about it, except let them know you love them.

Gwen and I live next to Somerville, New Jersey. It's an old New Jersey town that has a main street with a Norman Rockwell feel to it. The street is lined with shops, trees, and benches to sit on. Every Friday in the summer, they have an antique car show on Main Street. People from New Jersey and surrounding states bring their classic cars and park them along the street.

Leo would have loved this. Leo's passion was cars, and he would never miss a classic car show. Every time I walk down that street on a Friday, I think of him. It's almost like I can hear him say, "Hey, that sure is a sweet '67 Stingray." RIP William "Leo" Owens Jr. I bet you're driving the coolest red Mustang in heaven.

CHAPTER 21

THIS AIN'T WORKING

Joey and I did everything from private shows at exclusive resorts in Las Vegas to theaters in Rhode Island. We still fought like school girls, but our two-man show was going over really well. We were constantly getting compliments on how much people liked the fact that our show started with a guy from Mississippi followed by a guy from Brooklyn, New York. One night, we did a private show at a country club in Chatham, New Jersey. Joey thought it would be a great idea to have a female open the show because the audience would be all men who had just finished a day on the golf course.

As was often the case at private shows, the place wasn't set up for stand-up comedy. The sound system and lighting weren't good, and the general manager didn't understand the importance of getting everyone seated and quiet to start the show. When he introduced our opening act, everyone was still standing around, drinking and talking. She tried to talk over them, but they could barely hear her. The jokes she was telling about panty hose and menopause weren't helping get their attention either. While she was pushing through her set, I took a seat by a fireplace and started to resign myself to my fate. I figured if they couldn't hear her, they weren't going to be able to hear me either.

I was tired and I wasn't in the mood for this. Just as our opener was wrapping up, a thought popped into my head. Why don't I at least try to turn this thing around? I had survived everything from being the opening act for the wet T-shirt contest in Paduca, Kentucky, to the private show in Trenton, New Jersey, where a drunken hairstylist threw up on me in the middle of my act.

I decided if I was going down, I wouldn't be going down without a fight. I stepped to the microphone and yelled, "Hey fellows." That didn't work, so I yelled louder. A few people started paying attention, so I yelled even louder. I kept doing it until I had everyone's attention. I then said, "Be honest, how many of you would prefer a room full of dancing girls?" They said they wanted the dancing girls. I then said, "Well, that's tough because you're stuck with a redneck from Mississippi!" They erupted in laughter and all sat down and listened to the rest of the show.

We ended up having one of our best shows ever. As soon as Joey finished his set, he came over and told me how proud he was of me. He told me I had finally become a polished stand-up comic. As we were talking, a guy who was in the entertainment business in Manhattan came up and told us what a great show it was. He said we should start billing ourselves together. We should promote our act as the comedian from Mississippi and comic, magician, ventriloquist from Brooklyn. It sounded like a great idea, and we decided to do it. I thought we should continue doing our two-man show that everybody loved. Joey had other ideas.

He felt we would be better served if we developed a Dean Martin-Jerry Lewis style act with both of us on stage at the same time. We would even kick it up a notch with me having a ventriloquist puppet too, despite the fact that I knew nothing about ventriloquism. This was an idea whose time had not come, but I went along with it anyway. I started writing the material for our act and bought a hillbilly-looking puppet we named Emerson Bigguns. Joey knew the guy that ran Caroline's on Broadway in Manhattan because he performed there from time to time. The guy scheduled us to debut our show three months later on a Saturday night. I didn't know if this was going to work, but performing at the top club in New York City on a Saturday night was a great opportunity.

I found a small place to rent near where Joey lived in New Jersey so we could develop our act and prepare for the big night. These three months would be interesting. In the past, I would spend a few weeks on the road with Joey and then fly home to regain my sanity. Now he was two miles away and could pester me twenty-four hours a day. Every day he came up with some reason for us to do something. He would always say it had something to do with the show, but it never did. It would end up being a visit to a buddy in Staten Island or going to a magic store in Manhattan.

One of the more interesting trips was the time he told me we were going to meet some backers for our show, whatever that meant. I didn't know comedians had backers. I thought you just developed an act that people would pay to see and schedule shows at venues where they would pay to see it. I was right of course, but I went with him anyway. We drove over to Queens and turned into a neighborhood with modest houses. At the end of the street was a recently built house that was three times the size of any house in the neighborhood with a large security gate around it. That was where we were going.

We walked up and knocked on the door. When the door opened, I looked down to see a young kid who looked about ten years old. The kid was dressed exactly like Joey dressed when he did his act. He had the hat, tuxedo shirt, and black vest with matching pants. My first thought was that Joey had a son he hadn't told me about. No, it was more bizarre than that. This kid's idol was Joey, not Derrick Jeter or Eli Manning or any sports star whom kids in New York worshiped. This kid's hero and role model was Joey. He had done a show for the kid's dad and his associates a couple of months earlier. The kid saw the show and became Joey's biggest fan.

The actual reason we were there was the kid's mother wanted Joey to perform at the kid's birthday party, which was coming up in a month. For some reason, Joey was doing everything he could to get out of it. I didn't understand why he didn't just tell the kid's mother he couldn't do it, but I would find out before we left. He was hoping that he could spend the day teaching his protégé magic tricks and that would be enough for his mother to agree to Joey getting another magician to do the party. He wasn't having a lot of luck. Every time he would mention the other magician doing the party, she would get a concerned look on her face and say, "I don't know, Joey. All he talks about is you coming to his party."

As Joey taught the kid magic tricks, the reason he felt he couldn't just tell the woman no began to reveal itself. I looked behind the bar and saw twenty cases of Grey Goose vodka stacked in two rows. I wasn't the most worldly guy, but I knew that nobody buys twenty cases of vodka at one time. Even if he had a party every night, he wouldn't have bought twenty cases at one time. This looked to me, like it came off a truck and the driver might not have parted with it voluntarily.

I leaned over and asked Joey what this kid's dad did for a living. He got a serious look on his face and whispered, "Shhhhh, he's a made guy, a mobo." Beautiful, this would definitely fill up my bucket list of things I never intended to do. When I started this journey, I didn't think I would end up sitting in the house of a full-fledged member of organized crime. Well, "he" showed up a few minutes later. He was wearing a designer sweat suit with gold chains and looked like he could stuff somebody in a car trunk without breaking a sweat. He actually seemed like a really nice guy. We stayed for a couple more hours, and when we left, the guy told me if I ever needed anything to let him know. To be honest I thought about that for a minute. It might not be bad to have a buddy like that if I ever needed him. I quickly came to my senses and realized the last thing I needed was friends who listed "whacking people" on their resume.

Two weeks before our debut at Caroline's, we had a four-night gig scheduled at a club in Ohio. We were familiar with the club because we had played there several times before. We thought this would be a great place to rehearse our new act. We went over the material I had written each day leading up to the Saturday show where we would try it in front of a live audience. We would both do our normal sets and then I would come back on stage and join Joey at the end.

On the night of the show, he had been drinking heavily. This wasn't unusual and it never affected his performance, but I didn't think it was particularly helpful when we were trying to remember a new act. It wasn't. He didn't remember anything we had rehearsed. I saw it coming too. I texted Gwen right before I went back on stage: "We are about to go down in flames!" We did. I don't think the audience had a clue what we were trying to do, nor did the club owner. After the show, he told me I didn't need to be doing this.

He said, "You're going to make a great comedian, Pat, and you don't need no freaking puppet!"

I was beginning to think he was right, but we had a Saturday night show scheduled at Caroline's on Broadway and it was too late to back out.

The Wednesday before the show, Joey called as I was settling in for the evening. He wanted me to ride with him to Windsor Locks, Connecticut where he was doing a show for another comic. He said if I came with him, I could do a guest spot and the booker of the show would be there to see me. This is one of the oldest tricks in the book for veteran comedians. If they need a ride or just want somebody to come with them to drive back if they drink too much (which was Joey's case), they promise the guest spot. It rarely pays and you just end up going along for the ride. I was tired and it was five degrees outside, so I told him I wouldn't be going.

I called Gwen to tell her good night and told her about Joey asking me to go with him to his show. She said she had a feeling I should go. I thought it was nice that she was sitting back in Mississippi where the wind chill wasn't below zero, encouraging me to take a five-hour round trip to the middle of Connecticut. My problem was, when Gwen had a feeling, there was usually something behind it, so I called Joey back and agreed to go.

We walked into the restaurant where the show was being held, and the two comics who were performing in the show were sitting at a table. Joey introduced me to one of the guys, but he didn't know the other one. I introduced myself to the guy Joey didn't know, and we started talking. After talking to him for a minute, I realized I had met him before. It was John Larocchia, the guy I met on my last trip to the Hollywood Improv.

I did my guest spot, and it went great. The owner of the restaurant said having me show up was a pleasant surprise. John watched me too, which was good because he produced and booked a lot of shows in the New York area. After the show, John and I exchanged e-mails and phone numbers. There was a reason for me to come with Joey that night. I just didn't know what it was at the time.

The night of our big show at Caroline's finally arrived. When we got to the club, we saw the poster of us on the front door. When I looked closely at it, I realized it was designed by Joey. There was a huge picture of him and a very small picture of me. Instead of announcing both of us, it had his name in big bold letters and a line underneath that read, "With Pat McCool." The guy running the show said they were expecting a full house. This wasn't surprising because Joey said that in addition to inviting people that had seen us before, which was our initial plan, he had also invited people he personally knew.

I went back outside to call Gwen before the show. As we were talking, I was noticing people getting out of taxis and coming from the subway. I was starting to wonder if they were having a span-dex convention somewhere on Broadway. I then realized that if they were, they were holding it at Caroline's because that's where all that spandex was heading. I later found out Joey had invited half of his graduating class from Brooklyn. So now we were not only having the debut of our show, but also a high school reunion. That wasn't the only reunion Joey was having. He hired his former manager to host the show. Never mind the fact that the guy was not a comedian.

The show started with his former manager launching into a routine, which was to revolve around a guy he had planted in the audience. His plan was for that guy to reply to everything he asked with answers he had written down for him, which he thought would be hilarious. He thought wrong, because the guy he planted in the audience decided he wanted to be funny too. He purposely gave him the wrong answers just so he could watch him squirm. While this dog-and-pony show was going on the high school reunion was kick-ing into high gear, the last thing a comic wants to see is the crowd start to talk to each other. Once they get started, it's hard to get them to stop.

This crowd would be impossible to stop because many of them hadn't seen each other since their high school graduation. They were having a blast recounting their glory days and couldn't care less about what was happening on the stage. While this was going on, Joey was doing some catching up himself. He was holed up in the green room drinking himself silly with some of his old buddies. His former manager finally put the people who were listening out of their misery by ending his set. He then completely butchered the way we wanted him to introduce me, and I took the stage. When I stepped toward the microphone, he inexplicably reached behind the stage and handed me a different microphone than the one he was using. This caused the cords to get wrapped around the mic stand, so I spent the first minute of my set untangling the mess.

Within the first five minutes of my set, I almost got into it with one of Joey's former classmates, who was sitting on the front row making wisecracks about the state of Mississippi. He also made a remark about how funny I talked. One of the great ironies of life is having a guy from Brooklyn, New York tell me I "tawk" funny. I plowed through the rest of my set and headed for the green room. This was usually a glorious moment regardless of how my set went, because it meant the night was over. My night wasn't over, though. I still had to copilot this plane into the side of a mountain.

Joey was supposed to be waiting to take the stage as soon as I got off. Of course he wasn't, he was back in the green room getting sloshed. He finally got on stage and did his solo portion of the show. He then brought me back on stage for the grand finale. It was anything but grand. He didn't remember a single line we had rehearsed. He also added one final touch to this ten-car pileup by standing directly in front of me the whole time we were on stage. After the show, a friend of Joey's asked me to step outside. I had become friends with him myself. I liked him because he was a straight shooter and seemed to have a lot of wisdom. He told me I needed to stop this. He said I had a plan for my life and Joey was just throwing spaghetti against the wall to see what would stick. He said I could make it in the comedy business, but if I was going to do it, I was going to have to do it alone. He was right, and that was the last time I ever worked with Joey.

CHAPTER 22

WHAT A COINCIDENCE?

Joey didn't take the news of our divorce well. I didn't realize how bad he had taken it until I started contacting some of the club owners and bookers at the venues we had worked together. Many of these people had told me, without me asking, that they would love to have me back. One by one I got the same response. They seemed happy to hear from me at first. They would tell me to call back on a certain day when they did their booking. This is typical with club owners as they usually have certain days for that. When I called back, it would become apparent they had talked to Joey. They would then tell me to call back in a few weeks. I knew what that meant. It meant we would love to have you back but we've known Joey for fifteen years and he's asked us not to book you.

I was at a loss. In addition to what I was doing with Joey, my solo act was going over great in the New York area. I had just head-lined a show in New Jersey with over one thousand people. It took me over two hours to leave the place because audience members wanted to talk to me and take pictures. The guy who booked the show was thrilled with my performance and said he was scheduling me for future events. He was also a longtime friend of Joey, and those future events disappeared as well. It seemed like everything I worked for had turned to dust.

I sat around for a couple of months feeling sorry for myself. Things weren't supposed to work out this way. I truly thought I was doing what God wanted me to do. Now I felt like Graham Chapman in the Monty Python movie *Life of Brian*. It was about a guy, Brian, who was on the other side of the hill when God was telling Moses what he wanted him to do. Brian couldn't see Moses on the other side of the hill and thought God was talking to him. Unlike Moses, he didn't ask any questions and took off to do what he thought God wanted him to do. He showed up in Egypt a week after Moses had freed the Israelites and demanded pharaoh set them free. A dejected pharaoh told him the people had already left with Moses. Brian thought he was following the plan God set forth for him, but he was actually just bumbling through the desert. I was asking myself if God had truly sent me on this journey or, did I decide to do it on my own and just convinced myself he told me to do it.

One day, Gwen asked me if I wanted to go with her to our daughter Nicole's church in Brandon, Mississippi to see Jentezen Franklin. I had been watching him on TV for the past couple of years, which was kind of funny because the first time I saw him on TV, I told Gwen I thought he had shifty eyes. The more I watched him, the more I realized that he was awfully wise for a country boy from Georgia, with shifty eyes. Jentezen had become my go-to when I was on the road or wanted to skip church by convincing Gwen that my indigestion could be something serious. Since I was spending most of my time trying to figure out a reason to live anyway, I agreed to go.

When I saw him in person, I realized Jentezen didn't have shifty eyes after all. It must have been my TV. At the beginning of the service, my son-in-law Lee stepped onto the stage to sing. My wife had told me he could sing, but I wasn't prepared for this. I don't remember what he sang, but I got chills. Jentezen himself turned to the pastor of the church and said, "Where did ya'll find this guy" I knew I might be in for a special night.

Jentezen preached an uplifting message, but it was what he said toward the end that got my attention. I'm paraphrasing, but he basically said that God loves for people to take risks, step out of their comfort zones, put their faith in him, and follow the path he has set out for them. When I heard that, I thought to myself, "I know some people in here who have done just that."

He then looked in my direction and said, "God wants people in the entertainment business in Hollywood and New York. Not walking around hitting people over the head with a Bible but people who show God's love by how they act and treat other people." He really had my attention now. Who in Brandon, Mississippi could he be talking to? He may have been talking to the two elderly women sitting beside me, but I was convinced I was there because I needed to hear that.

My attitude changed overnight. I no longer felt sorry for myself because I knew the path I needed to take would reveal itself. The following week, I got an e-mail about a benefit comedy show in New York. It was from John Larrocchia. He was the guy I met on my last trip to the Hollywood Improv, and by an incredible stroke of coincidence, the guy I reunited with on my last trip with Joey before I left New Jersey. He was looking for comics to perform at a benefit they held every year for Hurricane Katrina victims. I immediately e-mailed him back and told him I was the guy for the show. I had been right in the middle of Katrina with my family huddled in the hallway while I watched large oak and pine trees crash through the roof of our house. A minute later, he e-mailed back, saying, "You're right. You got the gig!"

I was ecstatic. I wasn't going to make any money after I paid for my airfare and hotel room, but that wasn't the point. John booked a lot of shows in the New York area, and I felt if I did well, he would start using me in his shows. This was the opportunity I needed. On the morning of the show, I jumped out of bed, looked at Gwen, and said "I'm a comedian again!" I drove to the airport in Gulport, Mississippi, cleared security, and headed for my gate. They called for my zone to begin boarding, and I approached the gate agent. As I turned off the music on my phone, something told me to check my e-mail. The first unread e-mail was from John. He was telling me the show had been canceled.

I was stunned. I was just about to give my boarding pass to the agent as I read the message. I stepped to the side to figure out what I was going to do. There was no reason to get on that plane. I would just be flying to New York to sit in a hotel room. I turned around and slowly walked back to my car. I got in my car and called Gwen to tell her what happened. I then broke down and cried like a baby. The one character in the Bible I have always felt I was most like was Elijah. I'm not talking about the great prophet side of him. I'm talking about the other side. The side where he would be shouting God's praises for performing miracles one minute, then squalling under a juniper tree the next. My juniper tree was the parking garage at the Gulfport airport.

The following Sunday, my wife woke up and said she might not go to church because she wasn't feeling well. Usually when I heard this, I was back in the bed with my covers pulled up before she could finish telling me what was wrong with her. This Sunday was different. I felt as if I needed to go whether she went or not. I walked into church and took a seat next to my mother-in-law and father-in-law. I didn't realize the significance of this at the moment I sat down.

My father-in-law, W.L. Owens, is a retired Church of God pastor. He was a mentor to Don Hooper, the pastor of Destiny, the church we attended. He also had quite an influence on me. He supported us in everything we did. He's one of the wisest men I know and would always take the time to share that wisdom with me. The fact that I've grown to love and respect him is kind of ironic because when I first met him, I didn't care for him at all. He got upset with me because I wasn't holding on to a Visqueen properly. I didn't even know what a Visqueen was, but it's apparently a piece of plastic you use to cover appliances. I told Gwen at the time that I would be limiting my exposure to him from that point forward. It didn't quite work out that way as God obviously put him in my life for a reason.

My mother-in-law, Sarah Owens, was a different story. If I didn't like her, it was my problem because I don't think she has spent a minute of her life thinking about herself. If there are mansions in heaven, she's going to have one with a swimming pool, sauna bath, and a bowling alley. She has a direct line to God too. I can't count all the times she felt God's spirit was speaking to her about something that turned out to be true. I've told Gwen in the past it would be great if God would judge us all together.

I was sitting next to her, as Don delivered his message. I don't remember what the message was about, but it was stirring something inside of me. He got to the end and gave the invitation, which for some reason made me a little uneasy. I never felt the need to answer an invitation because I felt the prayer I prayed with the owner of the first insurance company I worked for had set me on a straight path to Beulah Land. Besides, as I had told my wife numerous times, I wasn't the type of person to display my emotions in public. She would laugh and say, "Yep, you are not emotional unless Southern Miss scores a last-second touchdown and wins a game you thought they were going to lose. Then you start bear hugging every total stranger within ten feet of you."

Well, I didn't raise my hand and nobody else did either, so I was relieved because I thought it was time to go home. I didn't realize that I had only survived round one, because Don did it again. I now started feeling very uncomfortable and was thinking, "C'mon, man, let's wrap this up and get out of here before I miss the first quarter of the Saints game." Nobody raised their hand that time either, so surely it was time to put an end to this. He then did it a third time, and I broke out into a sweat. I wanted to jump up and say, "Look, Don, every heathen in here who needed to get something off their chest has already done it, so let's call it a day." He had no intention of calling it a day until the person he was waiting on made a move. I didn't know that person was me.

Before Don got halfway through the fourth round, without even thinking about it, my hands shot up in the air and a feeling came over me like no drug I had ever taken in my life. Don shouted out loud in a way I had never heard before. I collapsed in my seat, and tears started pouring out of my eyes. I glanced over at my mother-in-law. She had the biggest smile I had ever seen on her face. I then realized there was a reason I came that day, a reason I was sitting next to her and from that point forward a reason for everything that would happen in my life.

Three days later, I got an e-mail from John Larocchia. He said another comic had to pull out of an upcoming show and the spot was mine if I wanted it. I did. I flew into JFK three weeks later and took the train to Wantagh, New York on Long Island. It was an annual fundraiser for the volunteer fire department. He did these shows all over the New York area to help raise money for the local volunteer fire departments. These are people who give up their time and risk their lives for their community. You can't walk into one of these fire departments without seeing a case in the lobby with the gear of fire-fighters who have given their lives for their neighbors. These are great people, and this was a great place to show John what I could do.

I had one of the best shows I'd ever had, and John was thrilled. He told me he had plenty of work for me if I wanted it. The other comedian on the bill was Joe Bronzi. He had a great show himself. We met backstage after the show and hit it off immediately. He offered to give me a ride to the train station, and we had to walk through the crowd to leave the building. When they saw us coming through, they stood up and applauded as we walked to the door. We walked through that crowd grinning like Cheshire cats and formed an instant bond along the way. It was a bond that would pay off in many ways.

Not only would we become good friends but he was going to introduce me to numerous people in the entertainment business who were going to help me in big ways. He also taught me an important life lesson that I will never forget. If a friend asks you to help him move from Philadelphia to New York and says he only has one small U-Haul full of stuff, he's lying through his teeth. Just say no and don't take his calls until you know he's finished moving.

That one show in Wantagh would lead to all the stand-up comedy gigs I wanted. Joe would introduce me to Mark Riccadonna, who would get me shows at theaters and clubs in New York City. Joe also hooked me up with a well-known comedy booker who booked me at clubs, private shows, and casinos. He also gave me every gig he was offered but unable to do. John booked me in just about every show he had. He also made me a featured comic in his Laughter Saves Lives national comedy tour. I also met Richie Byrne while working for John. Richie is the warm-up comic for the Dr. Oz show. He recommended me to his manager. She booked me in numerous clubs throughout the northeast. John also introduced me to Butch

Seltzer, who hooked me up with Roger Paul, who is one of the top bookers in New York. Roger has booked me in clubs, theaters, and private shows all over the country.

I went from being at a dead-end in Mississippi to not only going back to a full schedule, but also playing venues I never had the chance to play before. All of this from one e-mail that stemmed from one coincidental meeting. When I flew out of Los Angeles on my last trip to the Improv, I was convinced all my trips there had been a big waste of time and money. Other than a few great sets and a cool story about meeting Jerry Seinfeld, I thought I had nothing to show for it. I thought wrong, because on my last trip, that *something* inside of me that I have felt since the day I decided to become a comedian told me to walk back into the Improv one last time. That was the moment I met John Larocchia. Two years later, on a freezing winter night, as I was about to go to bed, that something stirred inside of me again and told me to take one last trip with Joey where I just happened to run into John Larocchia.

The chances of a guy from Mississippi being at the exact time and place that he needed to be for a coincidental meeting in Los Angeles and Connecticut are astronomical. That is if you believe in coincidence. I don't anymore. It was no coincidence that I ran into John when I did. It also wasn't a coincidence that I was working in Columbia, South Carolina at the Comedy House Theater at the same time as Joey. I was actually supposed to be there a week later but for some reason called Julie and asked her if I could move up a week.

All the times I had depended on myself to meet the right people, perform at the right club, and be in the right place at the right time had led me to the parking garage at the airport in Gulport, Mississippi. Fortunately for me, God had been working too. He knew I would be in West Hollywood and Windsor Locks, Connecticut, at the same time as John. He also knew which week I needed to be in Columbia, South Carolina. He knew where I needed to be and when I needed to be there. He just needed me to know that he was handling the things I couldn't. He also needed me to let go of the reins and acknowledge that I needed him to take charge of my life. That's exactly what I did the day that I was sitting next to my mother-in-law at Destiny church.

CHAPTER 23

AMAZING GRACIE

I was on a seven-day road trip to Alexandria Bay, New York. I was only performing Thursday, Friday, and Saturday, but it took me two days each way to drive from Mississippi. Alexandria Bay is a small resort town in upstate New York at the mouth of the St. Lawrence River where it empties into Lake Ontario. The area is also known as the land of a Thousand Islands, where the salad dressing I discovered tasted great on a bologna sandwich in a jail in Columbus, Texas, got its name.

I called Gwen from my hotel in Virginia on the first night of my trip. She told me about a dog she had seen on the side of the road in a timber lot on the way home from her parent's house in Marion County, Mississippi. There was one dog that had been run over and was deceased and the one she was telling me about was staying close by it. I had no idea why she was telling me this. I didn't need to hear some heartbreaking story about a lost dog who wouldn't leave its deceased friend or sibling and we sure as heck weren't taking in another dog. By that time in our marriage, we had already been through about fifteen dogs and five cats because she couldn't look at a stray animal without bringing it home.

She even once rescued a neighbor's dog that wasn't lost. She "found" a "lost" pug on our street and brought it inside because it needed a good home where it could get five meals a day. The problem was, the dog wasn't lost. We found this out two months later when the kid from around the corner knocked on our door and asked if we had seen their dog. I asked her what he looked like. She pointed to the dog standing behind me in our foyer and said, "Him." The dog would break out and come spend the night with us every chance he got, until they sent him to live with his "uncle" where he had plenty of space to roam.

We actually had three dogs because of another unnecessary rescue. On the day of Hurricane Katrina, Gwen and our daughter Devon saw a dog wandering through our yard. Right on cue, the Mother Teresa of dogs decided it needed a bowl of spaghetti. She fed the dog, and we made a bed for her in the storage room of our garage to ride the storm out. Hurricane Katrina eventually moved on, but the dog didn't. A month later, a couple of guys took down the large oak tree that had crashed through the roof of our house. One of the guys asked me if that was my dog now. I asked him what he meant, and he told me the dog belonged to his cousin who lived on a farm through the woods that bordered our subdivision.

The dog obviously just preferred living in a bigger house where they served home-cooked meals. A couple of weeks after that, we noticed the dog was gaining weight. I didn't think much of it because that will typically happen when you go from a bowl of dog food to five square meals a day. A few days later, we realized it wasn't Gwen's buffet that was causing her to gain weight. She was pregnant. She had three puppies, and we gave one to Devon's best friend. We kept the other two, so that left us with three and we did not need a fourth. Each night while I was in Alexandria Bay, we would have the same conversation. She would tell me she saw that dog again and it still hadn't left. I would tell her that it probably lived nearby and would eventually go home.

The three nights at Alexandria Bay went well except for the dreaded second show on Friday night. Most people think the second show on a Friday night would be one of the best shows for a comedian. They would be wrong. For comedians, the second show on a Friday night can sometimes stop just short of hand-to-hand combat. For the average person, there are three stages of drinking. The first is when you meet up with friends, have a cocktail, and everybody is glad to see one another. The second is after you've had a couple of drinks, everybody is in a great mood. The third is when you've had too much to drink and you start blaming your friends for all the problems in your life. That's the condition most people show up in for the second show on Friday night.

I knew we were off to a rough start when the doors were opened for the show. The first woman in line tripped over the doorstep and face planted in the doorway. The next three people piled up on top of her. The show was actually going well until I started into my bit about how I had been married twenty-five years and never cheated on my wife. This obviously struck a nerve with somebody in the audience because a ruckus broke out at a couple of tables to the right of the stage. I worked my way through it and finished the show.

As I walked through the lobby after the show, a guy walked up and started yelling at me. Through his slurred speech he said, "Thanks, man, I've been married for fifteen years and now it's all ruined because of you!" I apologized for wrecking his marriage and headed for the door.

The next day, as I was walking down the street, I saw a police car parked by the intersection. The police officer sitting behind the steering wheel was none other than the formerly happily married man whose life I had ruined the night before. I made sure to drive the speed limit as I left town the next day.

As I drove home on my last day of the trip, my wife was at it again but now she was kicking it up a notch. "That dog is still there and it's starting to break my heart" I'd seen the master of mission creep in action before and I knew where this was heading. I told her first thing the next morning we would go check on the dog. I rolled out of bed the next day in a fog from my trip to see her fully dressed, sitting in a chair and ready to roll. The sun was coming up as we turned onto the road where she had seen the dog. She leaned forward and scanned the woods intently as we slowly drove down the road.

"There they are! There's those ears! I always see its ears sticking up over that wood pile."

We stopped and got out, but the dog ran off. We could tell it was about an eight-week-old female puppy who hadn't been eating much. We couldn't tell what kind of dog it was, but she looked just like the one it had been staying with on the roadside. I didn't know if she had been abused or was just scared of people, but she wouldn't come close to us. We tried for over an hour to get her to come to us with no luck. She was watching us because we were near the other dog, but she didn't trust us. I decided to go to McDonald's and get a bag of hamburgers to see if that would entice her. It did to an extent. She would come get the piece of hamburger as long as I threw it across the ditch that was between us, but if I held it in my hand, she would just stare at me.

I sat on that roadside for over seven hours trying to get her to cross that ditch. Several people stopped and told me they too had tried to get the dog to come to them, but she wouldn't budge. According to the passersby, that dog had been there for almost ten days living in the woods in the middle of winter with no food or shelter. She had made up her mind that she wasn't going to leave the other dog, and I made up my mind that I wasn't going to leave her. I remember saying to her, "If you will just come across that ditch and trust me you'll have all the food you want and sleep in a warm bed. I don't know what happened to you that makes you scared of me, but if you will just trust me, you'll have somebody love and take care of you the rest of your life."

As it started getting late in the day, it became apparent I was fighting a losing battle. She wasn't coming, but I wasn't going either. I had locked eyes with that dog and decided she was coming across that ditch and going home with us one way or the other. I started to make plans to get a sleeping bag and build a fire. I was going to stay there as long as it took. Then I remembered I had a large kennel around the corner at my in-law's house. If she wouldn't come on her own, I was going to have to get creative. Gwen went to pick up the kennel while I continued my stare-a-thon with the dog.

When she got back, we set the kennel on the side of the road where I had been sitting. I opened the gate and tied a long rope to it and threaded it through the back of the kennel. I showed her a hamburger and tossed it into the back of the kennel. I then walked about fifty feet down the road and waited. At first she didn't take the bait, but after a few minutes, the smell of that burger got the best of her and she made her move. She sniffed around the kennel for a minute then stuck her head inside. A few moments later, she stepped in to get the hamburger. I yanked that rope and slam! She was ours.

For the first week we had her, she was still scared to death of us. Slowly but surely she learned to trust us. We would let her out to walk around each day as we cleaned her kennel, but she would always try to hide. One day, Gwen said, "Look." She was sitting at her feet and not trying to get away. When I put her back in the kennel, she started barking to get out. She was ready to join the family. As she continued to grow, we finally discovered what kind of dog she is. She's a rare breed called an American Dingo or Carolina dog and looks almost just like the dingoes that run wild in Australia. We thought it was amazing that she could live on that pile of wood we found her on for ten straight days. We also thought her loyalty to the deceased dog she wouldn't leave was pretty amazing too. So we named her Grace, as in Amazing Grace. Amazing Gracie now rules the house and sleeps in the bed beside me.

CHAPTER 24

I DON'T WANT TO GO TO NINEVEH

Eventually, living in Mississippi became a problem. I was starting to miss out on opportunities. I got a call one night telling me I had been hired for a commercial with a major sports network. I just had to show up in lower Manhattan the next morning at nine o'clock. That wasn't happening since I was in Mississippi and didn't have a private jet warming up at the airport. I had also recently missed out on some other great opportunities as well because I was 1,200 miles away. It was becoming apparent that if I was going to be in the enter-tainment business, I needed to be where the entertainment business was. We never considered moving in the past because the kids were still in school. This wasn't the case anymore, so we could move if that's what we needed to do.

I had two problems, though. The first was I didn't want to live in New York. I loved the city and I liked being there. I just didn't want to live there. I always thought I would be moving to Los Angeles. Not that I liked Los Angeles more than New York, it was just that I could handle Los Angeles. First of all, Los Angeles is warm. Secondly, I could drive down the street in West Hollywood and pull over to catch my breath if I needed to. When you walk out of Penn Station in New York, you better be moving or you will get trampled. It's like stepping into the street in Pamplona during the running of the bulls. I also didn't care for being stranded at a train station in the middle of the night with a wind chill factor of below zero. It took me almost three days to get the feeling back in my hands and feet. Gwen said she had a feeling God wanted us to move to New York. I told her to keep that feeling to herself because it wasn't in my plans. She then told me the story of Jonah in the Bible. God wanted Jonah in Nineveh but Jonah wouldn't go on his own, so God put him there. Well, I had no desire to find out what the inside of a blue whale looked like so I changed my plans.

Even though I decided we needed to move, my second problem was much bigger than my first. How in the world could we move to New York with our mongrel hoard? Most people won't rent to you if you have one or two dogs, much less four. The fact that Gracie looked like she could consume a human in one sitting didn't help either. I told Gwen if God wanted us to move, he would have to find a way for us to do it. He did. I got an e-mail from the guy from whom I had previously rented the small apartment in New Jersey when I was working with Joey. I hadn't talked to this guy in over a year, but for some reason he was asking me if I needed a place to rent. I e-mailed him back and said I did, but I have four dogs. I told him if that was a problem I would understand, but if it wasn't I was interested. He not only said it wasn't a problem but the house had a two-acre yard and was surrounded by woods, so it would be perfect for our dogs. Just like that, we were moving to New Jersey, twenty miles outside of New York City.

When we arrived in New Jersey, we still had one concern. The house had a huge backyard and woods on one side, but we had neighbors on the other side. Towns in New Jersey can be pretty strict about people controlling their pets, so if these weren't nice people, we could have a problem. Our dogs aren't just dogs either. They are "dawgs" that bark at everything that moves and never pass up the opportunity to hassle a human being. We quickly found out that these people were the nicest neighbors we have ever had. Joseph and Sylvia Pavlik who have two young sons, Joseph Jr. and Sammy. It seems they were just as concerned with their little angels wreaking havoc on us as we were about our dogs wreaking havoc on them. Another amazing coincidence, we had the perfect place with the perfect neighbors.

The week after we moved in, I had a show in upstate New York. It was about a three-hour drive, so I was driving up and back the day of the show. As the day got closer, they started forecasting heavy snow. It looked like the snow would come in late afternoon, so I decided to leave around noon so I would get to the venue before the weather got bad. The snow came early. I was in the shower around eleven o'clock when Gwen said I better look outside. There was already five inches of snow on my car. I got ready in a hurry and took off. As I got about twenty miles up the highway, the snow started falling heavier, but that was the least of my problems. The sound that I had been trying to ignore on the right side of my car couldn't be ignored anymore. My tire was flat.

I was now stuck on the side of the highway in one of the worst snowstorms the area had seen in years. I was already dressed for the show, so I decided to call roadside assistance to come and fix the flat. Bad move. They sent the worst roadside repairman in the history of worst roadside repairmen. First the guy got lost, then he had car trouble, then he had a bad case of diarrhea, which caused him to abort the rescue mission altogether. It was just as well, because by the time he called to inform me his battle with dysentery was more important than my flat tire, the snow plows had buried me under the snow. This is exactly why I didn't want to come to Nineveh. Not only was I going to miss a nice paycheck, I was now fearing for my life on the side of Interstate 287. After seven hours of shivering on the side of the highway, a tow truck finally stopped and pulled me out of the snow bank.

Not long after we moved, I had a weekend off. It was around nine o'clock on Friday night and I was just settling in. The phone rang, and it was my daughter Marlee. I answered the phone and asked her what was up.

She said, "Dad, Mike is dead!"

I sat in silence as I tried to get my mind around the fact that she had just told me my brother was gone. I was stunned, but I was not surprised. I gathered myself and asked her what happened, although I was pretty sure I already knew. She said they found him in his room. He had apparently died in his sleep. He had lost a battle that he had been fighting for years. Some people win their battles with alcoholism and addiction, some don't. Mike tried, but couldn't do it.

This wasn't supposed to happen. When I was doing everything wrong as a kid, Mike was doing everything right. He married his high school sweetheart and started a successful business. His future looked bright, but somewhere along the way it turned dark. He was a unique guy and never followed the crowd. His favorite hobby was Grand Prix racing, and his favorite driver was Nikki Lauda. He also couldn't pass a stray dog without picking it up and taking it home. He once found a dog on the side of a road that had been badly injured by a car. He spent thousands of dollars to save that dog's life. He named him Villeneuve after Gilles Villeneuve, the Grand Prix race car driver who had died in a crash several months earlier. He was always there for me. I wish I could have been there for him. RIP Michael Terry "Smoove" McCool. I hope you've had a chance to take a spin with Gilles.

I didn't get stuck in any more snowstorms, at least any I wasn't prepared for. I learned how to deal with black ice too, stay off it. I only needed my derriere to slam onto the asphalt one time to figure that out. I now set my sights on getting on TV. I hired one of the best acting coaches in New York City and started going on auditions. I hated going on auditions. I had performed stand-up comedy in front of every type of crowd imaginable, but for some reason, there is nothing more stressful than trying to remember two sentences for three people sitting at a folding table. Fortunately, the first role I landed only required me to remember how to say the word "yeah."

I got cast to play Ozzy Osbourne in a show for the Biography Channel. They dyed my hair solid black and told me it would wash out in a couple of weeks. They were lying. It didn't wash out at all, and I looked like a skunk for months as it grew back to its natural color. I got a few more TV parts but they weren't the type of roles I was looking for. I wanted to play the role of a guy from Mississippi who didn't belong in New York City and wasn't giving up immaturity without a fight. In other words, I wanted to play me.

I scoured the Actors Access and Backstage websites for months and that role never popped up. So I decided to create it myself. I had been encouraged by other comics to write a TV sitcom based on my abnormal life, but I knew nothing about creating and writing a sitcom. I also hadn't known anything about being a stand-up comic when I decided to do that, so I assumed I could figure this out too. I started working with a friend and fellow comic, Andrea, who had some writing experience. She was one of the comics who had encouraged me to create the show and was happy to help. After a few weeks though, it became apparent that I was writing a show about a guy from Mississippi but she was writing a show about a divorced Jewish woman from New York.

That might have been a funny show, but it wasn't what I was shooting for. She had also been working on her own TV show, so we decided it would be best if we did our own thing. I then decided I needed professional help, not the kind of professional help some might have thought I needed, but professional writing help. I needed someone to show me how to write a TV show, so I began my search.

I contacted one of the top writing groups in New York City to see what they offered. They had TV writing classes that I could take, but I decided against that. I had never been able to pay attention in class and had no reason to believe that had changed. The woman I spoke with also said they had private tutoring, which was exactly what I was looking for. She said I would pay a fee up front, then an instructor would be assigned to work with me. Just as I started to give her my credit card number, something told me to wait, so I told her I would call back. I decided to make one last search on the internet before I pulled the trigger.

I Googled "TV writing help," which I had done several times before. This time, the first thing to pop up was a picture of a guy teaching a class of about thirty people. His name was Al Zatkow. I had no intention of taking whatever class he was teaching, but something told me I needed to try to contact him. I found his e-mail address on his website and e-mailed to tell him what I was looking for. He got back to me and said he would be happy to help, so we set up a meeting in Manhattan. He lived in Brooklyn and I lived in New Jersey, so we decided to meet halfway. We picked the Cafe Java at the Port Authority in Manhattan. This would be our office for the next six months.

We were going to meet once a week for an hour, and I would pay him around one hundred dollars per session. I figured we would knock this out in about a month. I was wrong. Our first meeting was supposed to last an hour, but we talked for about five. He told me to write down what the show was about, including the main characters, and bring it back to him. He explained to me what a show bible was and how we would put it together. A show bible is what you use to pitch a TV show that lays out everything and every character the show is about. We would then use the show bible as a guide to write the pilot.

To write a show bible, you start by writing over one hundred pages, which gets condensed down to around thirty. You then condense all that down to two paragraphs into what is called the one page or elevator pitch. You need this in case you bump into a studio executive at Starbucks and want to sell them on your idea before their double latte Frappuccino is ready. You also need it because they apparently have the attention span of a gerbil and that's all they're willing to look at to decide if they want to hear more.

Gwen and I would write what Al told us each week, and I would bring it to him to polish it up. She has helped me do everything since the day we met. She took care of my policy holders when I was an insurance agent, managed the office when I supervised over fifty sales agents, and even helped me write my first five-minute comedy set. We did this for about six months, which was about five months longer than I originally thought it would take. I was beginning to think Al was just dragging this out so he could get a free iced coffee and one hundred dollars every week. That changed when Al started one of our meetings with a proposition.

He said, "Look, I've helped write over one hundred TV shows and feature films and I have to tell you, this is the best one I have seen." He then told me if I would be willing to give him co-writing credit, he would do the rest of it for free and show it to a producer with whom he worked when we were finished. I thought that was a great idea. We shook hands, and from that day forward I made him pay for his own iced coffee.

It took us over a year to finish the show bible and pilot script. As the year progressed, I became confident God had placed Al in my life for two reasons. The first was that he was the perfect person to work with to develop my show. The second was that I had a few other things I needed to work on: my ego, my pride, and my patience. Al pushed all three of them to their limit. I would write what I thought was the funniest stuff in sitcom history, and he would take it out of the script. I would put it back, and he would take it out again. I insisted on everything being funny, and he insisted on telling a story along with it. We argued over everything from the opening scene to what brand of salami one of the characters would pull out of the refrigerator. I would get so mad I wanted to drive to Brooklyn and choke the life out of him. It's a good thing I didn't, because I wouldn't have lasted a day at Riker's Island, and we ended up writing a really funny TV show. We named the show *McFool.*

The name *McFool,* we thought, was appropriate for our sitcom because people still have a hard time believing I gave up the life I had to become a stand-up comedian. Al sent the show bible and pilot to the producer Marc Henry Johnson, with whom he co-wrote the original pilot for the new HBO series *The Deuce*, which stars James Franco and Maggie Gyllandhall. Marc is a producer on *The Deuce* and brought the original concept to David Simon, the executive producer of the show. Marc has also won a Peabody Award. There are producers who have won both an Oscar and a Peabody who value the Peabody more. If we could get Marc to take the show, it would be fantastic. It would also save me the trouble of being ignored by every producer and studio executive in the TV industry.

We didn't hear anything from Marc for a while, which isn't unusual in the entertainment business. Apparently, people in this business are the busiest on the planet. I have no idea what they're doing, but I worked with one producer who was obviously so busy that she had to wait until two o'clock in the morning to send me an e-mail to tell me where I needed to be six hours later. I've also never understood why everybody in the business signs their e-mails with

"Best." I still don't know what that even means. Are they telling me it's the best e-mail they've written? Are they wishing me the "best" or just too busy to type "All the" in front of it? Whatever it meant, we just wanted to get one from Marc Henry Johnson telling us he liked our show.

We finally got that e-mail. Al forwarded an e-mail Marc sent him after reading our show bible and script on a flight from New York to Los Angeles. It said "*McFool* is great!" I didn't exactly know what he was saying, but it sure sounded good. I would later discover that Marc is the master of brevity and will use the least amount of words possible to get his point across. What "*McFool* is great!" meant was that he really liked the show and wanted to option it as executive producer and pitch it to networks. I was thrilled! I didn't even care that he signed the e-mail with "Best."

I met Marc at his Tribeca apartment and signed the paperwork. A couple of months later, he scheduled a staged reading/screen test. He brought in actors so he could film us reading the full pilot script. It was obvious we had a funny script because the actors couldn't stop laughing as they read some of their lines. He called me the next day and asked me how I thought I had done. I said I would give myself a C. He laughed and told me I was being too hard on myself because he gave me an A plus. He said he had been to a lot of screen tests, and this was the best one he had ever seen. He also told me the real reason he had set up the screen test. He needed to make sure I could act before he started to pitch the show. Now that he was confident I could, he was ready to move forward.

Marc then had another producer who was interested in working on the show take it to Montel Williams. We had a recurring role written in the show for Montel and needed to see if he was interested. The producer said Montel was bouncing up and down in his seat as he read the script. He not only agreed to play the role, but he also wanted to team up with Marc as executive producer and help pitch the show.

Marc then invited me and Al to a party at Hudson Studios in Manhattan so we could meet Montel. This was a party that people in the entertainment industry held every year to help musicians who had fallen on hard times, particularly those in the jazz community. Macie Gray would be performing at the party, and the guest list had everybody from Sweet Georgia Brown to the Prince of Luxembourg. I would have no problem striking up a conversation with Sweet Georgia Brown if I ran into him, but I had no idea what I would say to the Prince of Luxembourg.

I met Al in the city, and we walked over to Hudson Studios together. As we stepped into the elevator, I noticed that the guy beside me looked familiar. He was familiar. It was the Lethal Weapon himself, Danny Glover. We glanced at each other, and I said, "Hey, Danny, how are you?" like I had known him for years.

He then said what sounded like, "Fine, how have you been?" as if we had actually met before. I don't know if that's exactly what he said, but it sounded close enough. When the elevator door opened, I made sure to walk out right beside him so people might think we were together. The only person there was a security guard, and I don't think he was too impressed.

I walked in and sat down next to Maria Bartiromo, who hosts a show on the Fox Business Channel. I wanted to strike up a conversation, but all I could come up with was, "Hey, what do you think is the best place to put my money, bitcoin or lottery tickets?" I decided to keep that to myself because we all know that lottery tickets have a much higher potential return on investment. As the party was winding down, Marc took me around and introduced me to people as "the guy that brought him that great show, *McFool*." I didn't get to meet the Prince of Luxembourg, but I was ready if I had: "Hey, Prince, I love your chocolate. I'll holler if I ever get that way, maybe you could hook me up with a room in the palace where I could crash for a few days."

Marc and Montel recently went to Los Angeles to meet with networks about the show. After the first meeting with a major network, Marc sent me a brief e-mail. It read, "Pitched several shows, and *McFool* was the one they liked best!" He called me as he was meeting with another network to ask how I would explain certain things about the show. I would have rather been there to explain the show myself, but this is the TV business, so you take what you can get.

Apparently, things went great in the meeting because it lasted for hours. When it was over, Marc called and said, "I think we have found our network." He then gave me some details of the meeting and concluded our call by saying, "Tell Gwen you are on your way!"

I don't know what "you are on your way" meant, but as far as I am concerned, I've been on my way. I've been on my way since the day I looked up and asked God if he was real, and he began to show me that he was.

CHAPTER 25

THAT'S BONSAI?

A number of years ago, I visited my mother. I haven't mentioned my mother much in this book because much of what I have written about was crazy, absurd, and even sad. There is nothing crazy, absurd, or sad about my mother. She was the perfect mom in every way. She devoted her life to her family and always put our needs above hers. She didn't want to move to Mississippi when Dad had his orders changed from his assignment at the Pentagon. She loved life on a military base. Wherever we lived, she was involved in everything from being a Cub Scout leader, member of the PTA, or a volunteer at the elementary school.

Three years after we moved to Hattiesburg, my dad received new orders to move to Minnesota. He would have also gotten a promotion to full bird colonel. Dad sat us down and asked us what we wanted to do. Mike and I wanted to stay, but I'm sure Mom wanted to go. Once again, she sacrificed what she wanted for us. She finally got rewarded for all her sacrifices when my little sister, Tracey, was born. She was born when I was ten years old, so after raising three rowdy boys, Mom finally had somebody she could relate to.

Tracey loved acting and singing, so she joined the Hattiesburg Civic Light Opera. This wasn't just a local dinner theater. It was directed by Robert Mesrobian, who had extensive Broadway experience. Tracey was in numerous plays and eventually got the lead role in *Annie*. I couldn't believe how good she was. I remember how proud I was of her and couldn't hold back tears when she brought the house down with her version of *Tomorrow*. Mom and Tracey did everything together. They traveled to Europe, visited the Von Trapp house from *The Sound of Music* in Vermont, and made Christmas trips to the Biltmore Estate.

On the day of my visit, Tracey and my mother were sitting in the living room talking. I walked in and sat down. My mother said, "Pat, tell us about God. Is he real?"

I didn't have any scripture to quote or passage in the Bible to point to. I just said, "Yes, Mom, he is. You know what kind of person I was, and you know what kind of person I am now. The only thing that changed in my life was my belief in the God of Abraham, Isaac and Jacob, and his son, Jesus."

She looked at me and said, "Yes, we know, that's why we are asking you."

I didn't know how important that conversation was until this week. During a phone conversation between Tracey and Gwen a few weeks ago, Tracey told Gwen the reason she believed in Jesus was because of me. This was very comforting to Gwen and me because Tracey had been fighting the same battle my brother Mike had lost several years ago. Tracey also lost her battle one week ago from the day I am writing this. RIP, Tracey "Tebby Do" McCool. I love you, and I'll see you soon kid.

No one would have ever imagined that the kid who caused so much worry and heartache in our family would be the one they would look to for the answer to the most important question of their lives. I don't know if I could have given them a better answer that day, but my mother now sits in church every Sunday and raises her hands in the air and my little sister is singing in heaven. If I'm part of the reason for that, I don't need to accomplish anything else in my life. The fact that they looked to me on that day let me know that I was truly on my way, on my way to fulfilling the purpose God has for me and wherever that takes me will be just fine.

I was in San Francisco a couple of months ago on a week-long acting gig. At the end of the week, when we were all saying our good-byes, a security guard I had gotten to know at the venue approached me. He closed his eyes and gave me a bear hug that almost lifted me off the ground. He said, "It was so good talking to you. You're about the nicest guy I've ever met." At first I didn't understand why he would say that. I had talked to him throughout the week like I do with most people I work with. I asked him about his family, where he was from, where he grew up, what he had done in his life and what his plans were for the future. I did say a little prayer for him too, but he didn't know it. I find myself doing this a lot. Without thinking about it, I'll look at somebody I'm either talking to or watching walk by and say, "Dear God, I pray for his or her salvation. I pray for their health and happiness, and I pray for you to bless them in all they do in their life."

I thought about what that guy said on my flight home the next day. It made me think of something the producer of the show said to me a few months earlier when we were doing the same production in Miami. He walked up, put his hand on my shoulder, and said, "Pat McCool, everybody's best friend." I had no idea at the time where that came from, but after thinking about what that security guard said, it started to make a little sense. I wasn't everybody's best friend, and I sure as heck wasn't the nicest guy that security guard had ever met. Years ago, I wouldn't have spent more than a minute of my time with somebody who I didn't think could help me in some way. It was just God using me to let him know that somebody cares about him and thinks he's an interesting person. That security guard made me realize how important it is for people to know that.

A few years ago, I took a road trip that would take me from Memphis, Tennessee to Kansas City, Missouri then on to Denver, Colorado. Gwen went with me because I would have some down-time between cities. I wanted to stop by Fort Leavenworth where we lived when I was in the third grade. Fort Leavenworth was one of my favorite places growing up, and I had told Gwen about my time there on numerous occasions. I wanted to show her the places I had talked about and let her see Bonsai, the huge hill that tore me up the day I tumbled down it.

We pulled up in front of the house where we had lived. The area hadn't changed much. The large horn was still on the pole by the baseball field. The creek that my brother Mike used to fill up with baseballs looked the same too. I pointed to show Gwen the window of my bedroom. I then turned to show her my childhood nemesis, the massive hill we called Bonsai. I had told her about this behemoth on many occasions. As we fixed our eyes on it, I noticed a slight grin on Gwen's face. I had seen this look many times before. It's the look she gets when she wants to laugh at me but doesn't want to hurt my feelings. She finally couldn't contain herself and said, "That's Bonsai?"

She said that because Bonsai was not a huge hill. In fact, it wasn't much of a hill at all. It was more of an incline that most grandmothers could probably skateboard down without much risk of injury. I was puzzled at first. What had happened? Did the New Madrid fault line shift and level that thing off? The answer was no. Bonsai really wasn't that big of a hill. It never was. I just thought it was at the time. Everybody has Bonsais in their life, things they think are much more formidable than they really are. I still have Bonsais in my life, but they don't scare me anymore. Once I realized I don't have to climb them alone, they've become speed bumps on the road to where God is taking me.

Finally, as I finish this book. I see our dog Gracie, whom we rescued from the side of the road sleeping peacefully beside me. As I look at her, I'm thinking back to the day we took her out of those woods. We had everything she needed in her life if she would just come across that ditch, but she was too afraid of us to cross it. Fortunately for her, we looked at her the same way God looks at all of us. We were going to wait as long as it took. God feels the same way about you. He will wait as long as it takes, and he will never give up on you, just like my own father never gave up on me. No matter what I did or how frustrated he became, he kept waiting for me to come across that ditch. God is waiting for you to come across that ditch, and he doesn't care what you have done. If he loves me and has a plan for my life after all the things I did, he loves you and has a plan for yours.

I don't know why we've lost the loved ones we have, as I'm sure many of you don't either, but I do know why I'm still here. I'm convinced I'm here because God wanted me to tell you my story. I believe he also wants me to tell you if you or someone you know is battling addiction and despair or if you have reached a point where you don't think life is worth living that I have been there too. I tried to take my own life not once but twice. Each time in one of those great coincidences of my life, someone showed up to stop me. I now know the reason for that.

If you will just do as I did all those years ago, look up and ask him if he's real. He will start showing you that he is. He will also show you he loves you and has been with you all of your life as he has been with me. He was with me when my car was flipping through the air upside down. He was with me when bullets were flying at my back from ten feet away. He's with me now and wants you to know that he loves you and you are here for a reason!

If you are reading this, I believe it is no coincidence. I believe he wanted you to hear the story of how walking away from him led me to a life filled with misery and insecurity, and how walking toward him has led me to a life filled with joy and confidence. Just don't be afraid to cross that ditch! I pray that God blesses you and everything you want to do in this life.

The End

In memory of my father, Lieutenant Colonel James Max McCool, who went to be with Mike, Tracey and the troops who have gone before him one month from the completion of this book.

Thank you for never giving up on me!

You were the nicest and friendliest man I ever knew and it is an honor to walk in your footsteps.

Artillery lends dignity to
what would otherwise be a
vulgar brawl.

About the Author

Pat McCool was born in Fort Benning, Georgia into a military family. His father was an army officer, and he spent his early years as a military brat travelling from post to post. Upon his father's retirement from the military, his family settled in Hattiesburg, Mississippi, where he became a notorious juvenile delinquent. Pat has never followed the typical path laid out by society, choosing instead to create his own. He overcame the bad decisions of his early life and became a successful business executive. After spending twenty years leading a normal life in the corporate world, he once again felt the need to step out of the box. He left his lucrative position with a Fortune 500 company to pursue a career in the entertainment industry.

He is now a comedian, actor and writer living with his wife Gwen and their dogs in the New York City area.

CPSIA information can be obtained
at www.ICGtesting.com
Printed in the USA
BVHW03*1614141018
529457BV00001B/4/P